Assigned

No More Procrastination
Launch Your Destiny
People Are Waiting

BELINDA ENOMA

Dunamis Press

© 2018 by Belinda Enoma

All rights reserved. No part of this book may be reproduced in any manner whatsoever without written permission except in the case of brief quotations in articles and reviews. Please do not violate the author's rights by participating, encouraging or supporting piracy of copyrighted materials.

Published by Dunamis Press
P.O. Box 337,
Chester, New York 10918
www.dunamispress.com

ISBN: 978-0-692-05398-0
Library of Congress Control Number: 2018930929

Visit the author's website at **www.istartandfinish.com**

Unless otherwise indicated, Scripture quotations are taken from THE HOLY BIBLE, NEW INTERNATIONAL VERSION®, NIV® Copyright © 1973, 1978, 1984, 2011 by Biblica, Inc.® Used by permission. All rights reserved worldwide.

The Living Bible copyright © 1971 by Tyndale House Foundation. Used by permission of Tyndale House Publishers Inc., Carol Stream, Illinois 60188. All rights reserved. The Living Bible, TLB, and the The Living Bible logo are registered trademarks of Tyndale House Publishers.

Scripture quotations marked (NLT) are taken from the Holy Bible, New Living Translation, Copyright © 1996, 2004, 2007 by Tyndale House Foundation. Used by permission of Tyndale House Publishers, Inc., Carol Stream, Illinois 60188. All rights reserved.

Scripture quotations marked MSG are taken from The Message. Copyright © 1993, 1994, 1995, 1996, 2000, 2001, 2002. Used by permission of NavPress Publishing Group.

Scripture quotations taken from the Amplified® Bible (AMPC), Copyright © 1954, 1958, 1962, 1964, 1965, 1987 by The Lockman Foundation. Used by permission. www.Lockman.org

Cover design by Tami Roos
Printed in the United States of America

ACKNOWLEDGEMENTS

- God has been really good to me and I must continuously give him thanks. Thank you Lord for your loving kindness and mercy.

- Thank you to my husband Ben for constantly giving me full support in all assignments entrusted to me by the Lord. I am very grateful.

- To my three children – you are the best! Thank you for lovingly accompanying me to implement kingdom assignments.

- To my destiny helpers – you know who you are! You have been tremendously helpful in the implementation of assignments, especially in territories outside my comfort zone.

- To my editor Lee-Ann, I appreciate your great insight and help in bringing this work to fruition.

- To my family worldwide, thanks for your love and support.

- To our ministry partners, locally and globally, thank you.

❦ CONTENTS ❦

You Are the Assigned 1
1. Your Assignment Has a Start and Finish Date 3
2. Your Assignment Has an Identity 6
3. Your Assignment Has a Divine Code 23
4. Your Assignment Requires Holy Boldness 34
5. Your Assignment Has Companions 41
6. Your Assignment Has a Mentor 49
7. Your Assignment Has Ordained Timing 53
8. Your Assignment Requires a Defined Platform 59
9. Your Assignment Requires Revelation 65
10. Let the Work Be Authorized 69
11. Your Assignment Requires Education 71
12. Fruitfulness is Non-Negotiable 74
13. Your Assignment Needs the Outstretched Hand of God 80
14. Don't Worry About Attacks 85
15. Your Assignment Requires Persistent Faith 92

You are Qualified to Finish 98
Destiny Reminders and Quotes 103
About the Author 106
Your Journal 107

YOU ARE THE ASSIGNED

This is about the assignment that God has entrusted to you.
The people assigned by God to carry out tasks.
This is about you, his beloved.
Every person has an assignment on earth.
As I travel around the world carrying out kingdom assignments, I have seen that many people misunderstand their roles in their assignment and divine mandate. You are not alone, because I have done it too. What did I do?

I pursued when I should have waited.
I waited when I should have pursued.
I spoke when I should have kept silent.
I kept silent when I should have spoken.
I implemented when I should have just birthed.
I launched when I should have implemented.

I have seen pastors behind pulpits in buildings when the pulpits should be the marketplace. I have seen people in the marketplace whom the Lord has called to shepherd a group of people. Many people travel life's journey unfulfilled because they do not know which lane they should operate from. Many crave the spotlight when their light really shines brightly like a caravan lamp from behind the scenes.

Often when God gives us assignments, we do not receive a blueprint and because we fear God, we do not want to walk in disobedience. Hence, sometimes we delay and procrastinate.

I have written this book, Assigned, to help you understand your divine mandate, to empower you to fearlessly be yourself and operate with holy boldness; to show you the role you should play, point you to the right path towards fulfilling your destiny and for you to walk in the path of Ephesians 4:11-13, which says:

So Christ himself gave the apostles, the prophets, the evangelists, the pastors and teachers, to equip his people for works of service, so that the body of Christ may be built up until we all reach unity in the faith and in the knowledge of the Son of God and become mature, attaining to the whole measure of the fullness of Christ.

The apostles were assigned in the Bible. Now you have been called by God with an assignment, but how should you, the assigned, carry it out? Beloved, turn to the next page and start reading. You are already equipped to start, and very qualified to finish!

Agape love, grace, and peace!

Belinda Enoma

One

YOUR ASSIGNMENT HAS A START AND FINISH DATE

There are many who prolong the task either because they do not understand the assignment, they enjoy one phase of the assignment and continue to dwell in it, or they are too afraid to finish it and start the next one.

Temptation in the form of conversations from people with good and bad intentions can prolong your assignment. What am I talking about?

There are some situations where, as you are about to close your assignment or even announce that it is time to move on, someone with good intentions brings enticing suggestions and alternatives to keep you in the same spot.

If you are not in tune with the Holy Spirit and do not operate with holy boldness, it is possible that you will remain in the same spot instead of closing out.

In my life, I have learned to be watchful of who I take advice from. For example, why seek the counsel of someone who has not been where you aim to be? I am talking about seeking advice from small-minded folks for tasks given to you by a big-minded God, the Creator of the whole universe.

As you proceed with your assignment, remember that God has already predestined the boundaries and habitations of your dwelling (Acts 17:26) and that there is a start and finish date assigned to you.

Sometimes God will hide you until a glorious unveiling for his purpose. It is during your time of "divine hiding" that you undergo a refining process and equipping for the assignment. You may not understand what is happening during that period, and may even think God has abandoned you, but that is a place of strengthening, determination, and persistence.

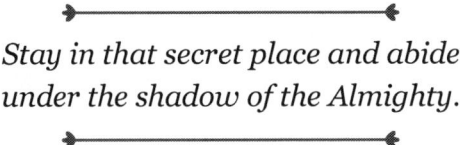

Stay in that secret place and abide under the shadow of the Almighty.

Your assignment can be a solitary place outside of your comfort zone. When God wants to elevate his servants or vessels, sometimes he will remove them from familiar surroundings and place them in places where they have no choice but to listen to him.

Elijah was at the Kerith Ravine, in the wilderness, but the Scripture tells us that the brook where he got his water from dried up after some time (1 Kings 17:7). The provision in your place of assignment has a start and finish time. Recognize the finish time so you do not dwell in frustration and question why God is no longer providing for you.

THE IDENTIFICATION PROCESS

Two

YOUR ASSIGNMENT HAS AN IDENTITY

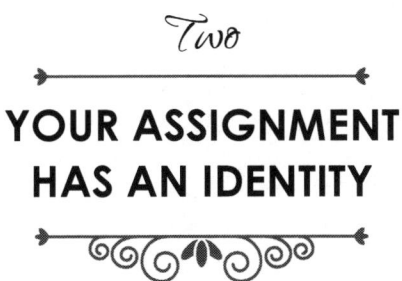

Your assignment has an identity. The way God created you is connected to your assignment. I have seen that some assigned by God to carry out his assignments hide their true identities for various reasons. This can create a less impactful experience, because people will not connect.

It is important for people to know your background so they do not fill in the blanks with explanations that can create rumors and strange guesses about you. If you hide yourself, those attached to your assignment will not connect because of the lack of authenticity.

Once upon a time, I shared somewhere that people in ministry should add in their biography; a bit about their history, or back story. That is, who ordained them, how they started, challenges they faced, etc. Someone said it was not necessary, especially because of connections and formalities involved with the ministries that ordained them.

The problem with such a statement is that too much formality can send people away. Besides, why would you need permission to add a known fact that is about your life in your biography? I am not saying that you should disregard bylaws of the ministry, but for the ordination to take place, it meant the ministry leadership concurred that God had a very important assignment for the assigned's life. They believed in his or her capabilities, gifts, and talents.

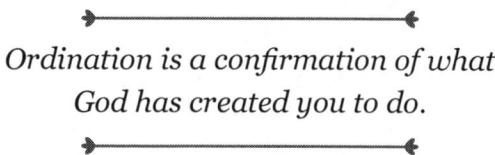

Ordination is a confirmation of what God has created you to do.

Do you need permission before adding in your biography that you graduated from a university or college? Isn't it part of your life story? As the assigned, do not give people any reason to doubt the call of God upon your life.

Do not hide who you are. There are people assigned to you who will connect with you just because of your back story, history, family, or ancestry.

THERE IS AN ASSIGNED LOCATION AND DESTINATION

Do you know that a specific location based on God's direction has been attached to your assignment? Sometimes we venture out on our own without fully knowing if the destination is appointed by God. Sometimes we even think it is definitely of God until we encounter issues, then we take a step back to really check if the journey was approved by God. That is not an easy situation to be in, especially in ministry.

However, we must not let fear enter. Here is my question for you: if you do not do what you believe is the right thing to do, twenty years from now, will you regret it?

Think about it for a minute.

Before I go out and minister to people, I am often reminded of the Scripture about the four lepers (2 Kings 7) who were in a dicey situation because the land was filled with famine. They said to themselves (in my paraphrased version): If we don't go and see, we die. If we go and see, we die anyway, so what's the difference? Let's just go and see!

They said to each other, "Why stay here until we die? If we say, 'We'll go into the city'—the famine is there, and we will die. And if we stay here, we will die. So let's go over to the camp of the Arameans and surrender. If they spare us, we live; if they kill us, then we die."
—2 Kings 7:3-4 NIV

This life is not our own; neither is the mission of our assignment. Whatever we do, we do unto the Lord. What do you have to lose when you walk in holy boldness, notwithstanding what you may face?

- Closed doors?
- Attacks from the opposition?
- Cold reception?

All closed doors are not caused by the devil. The Holy Spirit closes doors too, and no matter how anointed you are, if he closes the door, it is closed indeed! Wasn't Apostle Paul very anointed with signs and wonders accompanying him?

In Acts 16, we see that some doors were closed to him and his team. What is important in your assignment location is to stay connected to headquarters; that is, the Holy Spirit, and keep moving when one door closes. You do not stop, because it is not over until God says it is over.

YOUR ASSIGNMENT DOESN'T HAVE TO REMAIN WITHIN THE FOUR WALLS OF A CHURCH

Your assignment can extend to the marketplace as yourself—the real you—the one who fears God, believes in him, and is carrying out his mandate to "be fruitful and multiply." Do you know that some doors have refused to open because people are not sure of who you are?

John the Baptist's assignment (Matthew 3) was to preach in the desert (wilderness, his assigned location) and everyone came from all over to see and hear him there.

Note these three important things about John the Baptist:

- He knew his assignment.
- He knew his message and it was very clear: "Repent of your sins and turn to God, for the Kingdom of Heaven is near."
- He did not fret about the location or how he looked.

The Bible tells us in Matthew 3:4 that "John's clothes were woven from coarse camel hair, and he wore a leather belt around his waist. For food he ate locusts and wild honey."

He dressed weirdly and ate unusual stuff. Who eats locusts and wild honey for food every day? Yet, many people came from afar to see and hear what he had to say.

There are many today who are preaching in the palace when they are called to preach in the streets. God did not create you to have a confused destiny. It is imperative that you know your assignment location so you can fulfill your destiny.

Understand that the way you were created is connected to the assignment and location God has ordained for you.

Even though John's disposition matched his assignment location, his physical appearance did not matter. What mattered was what was in him: the message he carried, what he said, the baptisms, and changes that occurred.

The Lord desires us to rend our hearts and not our garments. He looks at the heart and not outward appearances. When we fully dive into our assignment location and walk in total obedience to God, things happen.

Did it matter that John was in the wilderness? No. It was his assigned place to proclaim repentance to the people, for the kingdom of God is at hand.

YOU HAVE AN AUDIENCE

Sometimes your assignment is for one person, a small group, or multitudes. Your assignment location has a recipient. Some will question your motive for jumping out of familiar territories when help is needed in your locale. However, what people do not understand is that your assignment has a destination with a specified audience attached to it.

> "For example, remember how Elijah the prophet used a miracle to help the widow of Zarephath—a foreigner from the land of Sidon. There were many Jewish widows needing help in those days of famine, for there had been no rain for three and a half years, and hunger stalked the land; yet Elijah was not sent to them."
> —Luke 4:25-26 (Living Bible)

Why didn't God send Elijah to the Jewish widows who dwelt there? Why did he send him to a foreigner instead? God has his reasons; all we must do is obey and carry out the assignment.

It is important to identify the group, person, or community you are called to reach. It is like personal branding. If you do not know who you are, the wrong people will follow you or become attached to your assignment. Hence, you run the risk of making no impact because they are not for you.

At this point in your life, do you really need that kind of unordained attachment? Does your destiny have time for it?

Your assignment in a particular location may produce miraculous results for only one person, a group, or everybody.

> "Or think of the prophet Elisha, who healed Naaman, a Syrian, rather than the many Jewish lepers needing help."
> —Luke 4:27

Again, why did God allow only one person, Naaman the Syrian, to be healed? We do not question God, we obey.

YOUR ASSIGNMENT CAN BE IN ONE LOCALE BUT TO MULTIPLE GROUPS

In Acts 19, Paul went on a missionary trip to Ephesus. Upon arrival, he met some believers who had never heard of the Holy Spirit. They believed in Jesus Christ, but they did not know everything.

As the assigned, it is easy to think that people know what you know. The reality is that they do not. Everybody is not on the same level. The believers at Ephesus were already baptized but it was "John's baptism," which was essential but not total.

> Paul said, "John's baptism was a baptism of repentance. He told the people to believe in the one coming after him, that is, in Jesus." On hearing this, they were baptized in the name of the Lord Jesus. When Paul placed his hands on them, the Holy Spirit came on them, and they spoke in tongues and prophesied. There were about twelve men in all.
> —Acts 19:4-7 (New International Version)

In the Ephesus experience, one of Paul's assignments was to believers. However, another thing happened. He did not stop there and say, "Praise the Lord! Twelve people have received the baptism of the Holy Spirit; my mission is complete. I can go now, happy that something great happened at Ephesus." What Paul did next was to face the synagogue.

> "Paul entered the synagogue and spoke boldly there for three months, arguing persuasively about the kingdom of God. But some of them became obstinate; they refused to believe and publicly maligned the Way. So, Paul left them."
> —Acts 19:8-9

REJECTION DOES NOT MEAN TO QUIT THE ASSIGNMENT

There are many strategies for the implementation of your assignment in the word of God. How about you pick one missionary journey of Apostle Paul and see how he carried out his tasks?

In Ephesus, he fearlessly talked about the kingdom of God and he faced opposition. Some of the people in the synagogue even spoke evil of the Way of Jesus; but Paul was there for three months. He did not leave immediately.

In times of opposition, do we quit easily?

Do you still try to get your message across or do you just leave because you do not have patience to share the Good News of Jesus Christ with people who do not want to listen?

BECAUSE ONE PLACE REJECTS YOU DOES NOT MEAN YOU SHOULD GIVE UP

> Do your part, and God will take care of the rest. You must continue and not allow the enemy's tactics in the form of fear to stop your assigned work. Paul did not stop there. He then went to "the school of a man named Tyrannus. In that place, Paul talked with people every day for two years. Because of his work, every Jew and Greek in Asia heard the word of the Lord" (Acts 19:9-10).

If Paul had left the location totally, do you think every Jew and Greek in Asia would have heard the word of the Lord? The Bible does not tell us that they were converted but they "heard." He went to a school and talked with them every day for two years.

If we assume that no conversion took place in Tyrannus' school, what about impact? On your assignment journey, the result you expect may not happen immediately; but do not forget the seed that you sow in that place because of your obedience. We know that faith comes by hearing, and hearing by the word of God.

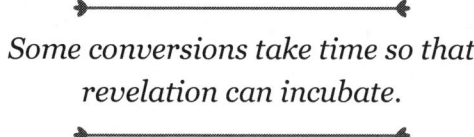

Some conversions take time so that revelation can incubate.

Every opportunity you have to deliver God's message in a location has a purpose. Don't miss it because of impatience. If you are a speaker and you are invited to speak in a city or country that is not familiar to you, use the opportunities available to you to share the Good Word. What do you have to lose? Time? If you lose time teaching the word of God, you elevate your legacy.

This is not about hustling for the next speaking engagement, but purposefully seeking out ways to boldly talk about Jesus that is aligned to your assignment in that particular location.

BE CONSISTENT IN YOUR ASSIGNMENT

Paul was consistent. He did not give up. The onus of his message was the same. Knowing who Paul was, it really was about Jesus Christ. Tell yourself, "I am in this for the long haul. This is not 'fly-by-night' but 'all the way.'"

Many miracles took place in that region and God used Paul mightily. There is power in exercising your faith to do great exploits. Refuse to be shaken by anything that wants to interfere with what you are ordained to do.

Did you notice the trajectory of Paul's movement in Ephesus?

First, it was **twelve people (small group)**. Secondly, it was the **synagogue (multitude)**. Thirdly, it was Tyrannus' school (**multitude**; assuming we go by the average number of people in schools today). He did not stop at twelve people; he kept going.

DESIRE IMPACT, NOT POPULARITY

If you ever host an event at church for your business or organization, if the expected numbers do not show up, be not discouraged. Even if one person attends and you pour into that person, a ripple effect can occur.

Once upon a time, I had an event organized for forty people in an unfamiliar territory but only two people registered. A couple of weeks before the event, I wanted to cancel and refund the fees because it just did not make sense to me to continue. There were huge costs involved, including the hotel venue that was already reserved and paid for. Besides, to proceed with the commitment meant traveling from out of state with my family, and everything else that goes with preparing for a conference.

God knows exactly what his people need and he will use whomever he chooses to carry it out.

As I sat in my office contemplating whether to cancel or not, my phone rang and it was someone who was registered to attend the conference. We had a nice chat, and I just knew that the event had to continue. I believed God that more people would sign up.

I declared by faith that they would show up, but it did not happen. Only the two registrants came, and I poured out everything the Lord had given me for that city into them as if I was speaking to one hundred people.

Were they blessed? Yes.
Was there impact? Yes.
Are they still walking in their purpose? Yes.
Was that assignment successful? Yes.

It was successful because it dawned on me that when children of God pray, he sends someone to them to help them out. The person being sent may expect a multitude, only to find a couple. I realized that the assignment was for just the two of them.

Should I have looked at it as an 'enemy attack' to frustrate my purpose? No. It was an assignment not based on numbers, but impact. Even if to the spiritual eye it was an attack by the enemy, he failed woefully. I delivered the messages and strategies. As usual, God got the glory.

I was reminded of Hebrews 11:8 (New Living Translation), which says:

> It was by faith that Abraham obeyed when God called him to leave home and go to another land that God would give him as his inheritance. He went without knowing where he was going.

When we focus on the "ifs," we begin to disobey God. Let us move by faith and trust God that in his infinite mercies, his purpose shall be made manifest.

In Acts 8:26-40, an angel of the Lord told Phillip to go along a desert road and Philip obeyed, even though the reason was not given to him. It was at that place that he met an Ethiopian court official who was reading Isaiah, and Phillip talked to him about Jesus. In your assignment, be receptive to the promptings of the Holy Spirit and embrace the detours he brings.

For example, if you are already on an evangelistic assignment, God may draw you out of the territory to a nearby place just for one person. Sometimes we miss our blessing because we crave popularity over impact. Do not let the quest for huge numbers derail your assignment or make you align with demonic agents whose sole purpose for connecting is misalignment.

BE OBEDIENT IN THE ASSIGNMENT

Your assignment has an audience to whom you must give the exact words the Lord has given for them. They must not be diluted to draw a following.

Sometimes instead of carrying out the Lord's assignment accordingly, delivering exactly what he says, the messenger dilutes the message to please the audience. The messenger allows himself or herself to be influenced by what the people say instead of impacting the people assigned to him or her.

There is a consequence for disobedience. If you haven't done what you are supposed to do, restoration is available to you right now, and this is what the Lord says:

> If you repent, I will restore you that you may serve me; if you utter worthy, not worthless, words, you will be my spokesman. Let this people turn to you, but you must not turn to them.

—Jeremiah 15:19

KNOW THE CULTURE

Before you approach your audience or integrate with them for the purpose of carrying out your assignment, understand the "culture" of the territory you are about to enter. Don't assume everybody is like you or behaves like folks in your neck of the woods. Do your homework.

Connect with people in your assignment territory who know the nooks and crannies of the place and educate yourself. Yes, you have the Word, you speak in tongues, you are a prayer warrior, but the Word also says:

> Any enterprise is built by wise planning, becomes strong through common sense, and profits wonderfully by keeping abreast of the facts.

—Proverbs 24:3-4 (TLB)

GOD CAN SHIFT YOU FOR ACTIVATION

Just when you think you are moving for your own good, helpers of destiny in the form of employers or leaders show up with offers you cannot refuse and help you pack and settle in a new assignment location.

It happened to me many years ago when I accepted a technology consulting position at a major corporation in Denmark. It was an excellent offer, and I thought I was going for my own financial prosperity, not knowing that the Lord had other plans. He shifted me for the activation of his assignment.

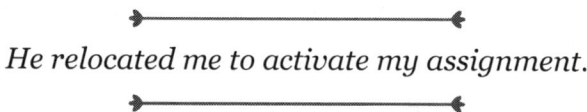

He relocated me to activate my assignment.

It was in that location that I received the baptism of the Holy Spirit. I was there on a work assignment and a huge crusade was taking place in Copenhagen. Was it by coincidence that I just happened to be there? No, I believe it was by divine appointment.

I was already a believer, and I received the Holy Spirit through the laying of hands upon me by a Dutch man of God who accompanied a Nigerian-American man of God on assignment to the Scandinavian region.

I often tell people during global ministrations that God can relocate you to activate your assignment, and that was what happened to me. He already knew what would take place in Copenhagen, but I did not know. It was later that it became clear to me why the job positions I applied for in other cities did not come through.

Initially I was upset because I was in between job contracts longer than I expected, but God was preparing the next location for me, customized for his glory. To the physical eye, it was an unnecessary delay. To the spiritual eye, it was a divine delay that required persistent faith and patience.

YOU CARRY CITIZENSHIP THAT OPENS DOORS

How can an assignment carry citizenship?

An assignment is not a human being, but a task. However, metaphorically, it can have citizenship because of its carrier—the person appointed by God to carry out his tasks.

Citizenship identifies the nationality and origination of a person.

Where do you come from? Where were you born? As you proceed with the implementation of your assignment, understand that it has citizenship. With citizenship comes rights, obligations, and social responsibility to a nation or kingdom.

As a vessel on an assignment for God who has placed something in your hands to be released on earth for his children, you must walk with kingdom power. On God's assignment, your heavenly or earthly citizenship can protect you from danger.

In Acts 22, when the commander ordered soldiers to give Paul lashes, he disclosed his Roman citizenship. The next day, he was freed from his chains.

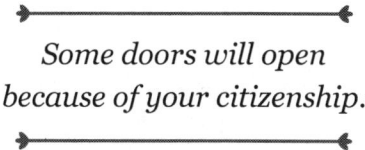

Some doors will open because of your citizenship.

The kingdom of God should not discriminate. However, there are times when your place of origin opens doors for you. There are some places only you can go because of your citizenship.

There are some people only you can reach because of your nationality. Whether you acquired citizenship as a birthright or through naturalization, your assignment shall connect you. God always invests in souls.

God will send you to some places because he knows that you have the right of entry into those territories. Doors will open for you to successfully carry out your assignment because of your citizenship.

Some people will listen attentively to your message because of your citizenship, so make use of your citizenship for the kingdom of God.

YOUR ASSIGNMENT HAS A LANGUAGE

An important part of carrying out your assignment includes doing some research about the territory you are about to enter. I have seen that an assignment has a *language*. Literally.

In your research, study the culture in that area. There is a specific expectation from the audience. I have also seen that people are more inclined to hear your story if you sound like them, or speak their language.

LANGUAGE AND POLITICS

An example of the power of language on assignments is politicians campaigning in certain areas. They want the people's votes, but do not understand the struggles of the people. The media has a great way of allowing the world to partake in politics and enable us to make informed choices.

You cannot be raised in affluence and be talking about saving souls in poor areas if you have not immersed yourself in the culture, or at least tried to understand their pain and struggle. The area has a language that you must understand before you embark on your assignment.

I recently heard a story about a preacher who went into a prison to minister to inmates. It was an operation that required holy boldness coupled with the uncertainty of a cold or warm reception. The praise report he brought back was that they received the message with gladness.

However, I do believe that his life experience helped his assignment too, because he was once incarcerated, fell on hard times, and knew their pain and suffering.

The story you share, whether in or from the Word or based on your life experience, has a language for a specific audience.

It is not a coincidence that certain folks are drawn to you because of how you are. How do you talk? What do you speak? Slang, patois,

English, Pidgin English, Igbo, Yoruba, Spanish, French, Creole, Greek, posh?

IT HAPPENED TO PAUL.

When the people heard Paul speak in Aramaic (Acts 22), they became very quiet and listened. Paul said:

> I am a Jew, born in Tarsus of Cilicia, but brought up in this city. I studied under Gamaliel and was thoroughly trained in the law of our ancestors. I was just as zealous for God as any of you are today...

This Scripture teaches us that your language and where you are from is important for the fulfillment of your assignment. In my own paraphrase, he is saying:

> I am one of you. I used to be like you. I was born in _____ but I grew up here. I know you. I understand you. I know your struggle, but this is my story and how my life changed.

Do not be offended if on your assignment journey some people refuse to listen to you because you do not speak like them. Some folks are drawn to what seems familiar. It is not always right, but it is human nature. Although familiarity has a connection, it is not necessarily safe or sound.

One of the benefits of familiarity in this type of situation is that it becomes a starting point—a door opener.

WHAT ABOUT THAT SPEAKER AT THE CONFERENCE?

If you were at an event and you heard two people speak, who would you listen to more: the one who spoke your language or the one who just talked and could not relate to your struggle?

Audibility and visibility are game changers. What is perceived at first sight can change the operation of a game. What is heard at first instance can grow or halt the reception of a message. They say you attract who you are, and that is not a lie. Pause and think about it for a minute.

Have you ever attended conferences where someone spoke a word and you wondered if he or she eavesdropped on your conversation? I have connected with people I heard speak because they "spoke my language." I am not talking about English or dialects, but themes that are dear to my heart.

They hit the nail right on the head and we had things in common. They understood me. I understood them. I followed them on social media. They followed me on social media.

Do not underestimate the power of your assignment language. It kicks open doors that otherwise would have remained shut. I often say that no experience is wasted.

Perhaps you are fluent in another language. Did you study French at school or Spanish? Did you do a study abroad program and immerse yourself in the culture? If you did, they are not wasted years. The second or third language you learned has a purpose. Get ready to deploy them!

DESTINY NOTE

Do you know your assigned place to proclaim the message God has placed in your heart? Have you considered your assignment identity? Do you know your audience? Do you know their language? Do you speak it?

THE KINGDOM DNA

Three

YOUR ASSIGNMENT HAS A DIVINE CODE

There is a code of conduct allocated to your assignment. For example, things shift when preachers understand that humility goes a long way and gratitude opens doors.

Things shift when people realize that pastors are project managers or branch managers. Our Boss is Jehovah and we report to him. Yes, you used the power he gave you to generate wealth and draw a following but it is grace; unmerited favor, Jesus Christ, the Lamb of God, that turned the tide, not you.

Once people are connected to your assignment, their lives change. Your assignment is not for decoration or for popularity. It transforms, edifies, and burns demonic altars.

Your assignment creates ripple effects in societies and nations. Do not underestimate the power that you carry. God has equipped you with a divine code that operates with the same power that raised Jesus Christ from the dead.

THAT CODE NEEDS INTERCESSORY PRAYER TO OPERATE WITH FIRE

Your assignment requires prayer; lots of prayer, and consistent prayer. You are never too busy to pray. One trick of the adversary of our souls is to make us feel that once God has answered our prayers, we do not need to pray with so much fire and passion as we did during expectation.

Understand that there is nothing the devil would like more than to take you out. He does not enjoy the fact that you are so determined to keep putting dents and even burning spiritual fire in his camps. Whatever you do, never relent in prayer.

Set time aside daily to pray. Set your alarm clock just as you would expect to wake up early to go to work. We do not like to be late for work or miss the train or bus or carpool, so why is it not a big deal when we miss personal prayer times?

As you proceed with your assignment in the church, business, workplace, or even (especially) within the government, pray several times a day. Make it a very important part of your schedule.

A prayerless vessel of the Lord can be easily attacked by the enemy.

The Lord releases strategies through prayer. I have seen situations where, during prayer, the Holy Spirit will reveal a particular Scripture verse. Then when it is read, the plans of the enemy become very clear.

I have experienced it.

As soon as our prayer session was over, the people the Lord revealed to me via Scripture to be wary of pressed our doorbell. And it happened as the Lord revealed it in the Scripture verse. I will never forget that experience.

It was literally after the prayer session with my husband that it happened. It warned us about backbiters and people who did not have our best interests at heart. The Holy Spirit also revealed to me that they would come and confess. Lo and behold, it was exactly as it was revealed!

> *The Word of God does not lie. Let us take our time to truly study it and apply it to our lives.*

THAT DIVINE CODE CAN OPERATE VIA DIFFERENT PLATFORMS

As the assigned of God, let us not rush because of time constraints, especially at certain locations. Thankfully, the Internet has made it easy to continue delivering God's messages beyond live events.

Embrace the platforms that the Lord gives. Hold virtual sessions, webinars, and virtual summits. The world is so huge, and we cannot reach everyone at once. However, whatever we teach can be replayed or rebroadcast via evergreen webinars.

THE CODE REQUIRES INTEGRITY

Balaam faced a strange situation. In Numbers 22, Balak, king of Moab, sent messengers to him to come and curse his enemies, the people of Israel. He was ready to pay Balaam for placing a curse on them. The Moabites were terrified of the Israelites because they had seen what they did to the Amorites.

> Balaam responded to Balak's messengers, "Even if Balak were to give me his palace filled with silver and gold, I would be powerless to do anything against the will of the LORD my God.

Balaam rejected Balak's wealth proposition. Beware of folks (especially people in high positions of authority) who will try to entice you with money to go against the will of God. Do not ruin your reputation or halt your destiny because of bribery and promises of wealth. If you operate in the prophetic, watch out for "pay-per-see" or "pay-per-curse" situations. Integrity is required at all times. Let us aim to please God and not man.

THE CODE REQUIRES YOU TO NOT SUBMIT TO ANGER

In your assignment journey, if you ever encounter a situation where someone bites the hand that has fed him or her (your hand), do not be moved to anger. It is what the enemy wants.

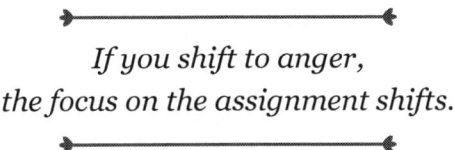

*If you shift to anger,
the focus on the assignment shifts.*

Once upon a time, I heard someone say that "ingratitude is worse than witchcraft." Initially I did not quite understand what the person meant, but as I got older, it became very clear. There is nothing as bad as when someone is very ungrateful, especially after giving to them sacrificially. I know the feeling and it is very annoying.

In 1 Samuel 25:2-38, David and his men needed help from someone they had previously helped but the man, Nabal, was crude and mean. David sent his men to him and they delivered this message.

> While your shepherds stayed among us near Carmel, we never harmed them, and nothing was ever stolen from them. Ask your own men, and they will tell you this is true. So would you be kind to us, since we have come at a time of celebration? Please share any provisions you might have on hand with us and with your friend David.

Nabal's response was not one expected from someone whose men were helped by David's men, who even served as a wall of protection for them. David was furious, and made a decision to destroy him because he repaid him evil for good. When Abigail, Nabal's wife, heard of this evil response of her husband, she took matters into her own hands and went to David.

> She quickly gathered 200 loaves of bread, two wineskins full of wine, five sheep that had been slaughtered, nearly a bushel of roasted grain, 100 clusters of raisins, and 200 fig cakes.

Upon arrival, she begged David and told him, "Don't let this be a blemish on your record. Then your conscience won't have to bear the staggering burden of needless bloodshed and vengeance" (1 Samuel 25:31 NLT). David accepted her present and thanked her for keeping him away from murder and carrying out vengeance.

Vengeance really belongs to the Lord!

If Abigail had not stepped in, perhaps David would have killed Nabal and taken matters into his own hands. He did not have to do that because when Abigail told Nabal that she went to see David, something terrible happened to Nabal. "He had a stroke, and he lay paralyzed on his bed like a stone. About ten days later, the LORD struck him, and he died" (1 Samuel 25:38).

The Bible tells us that vengeance belongs to the Lord and he will repay. When people do evil to you, including those you have bent over backwards for, don't worry. Let God handle the situation.

Don't be tempted to enact revenge and mess up your assignment. Don't be provoked to anger, because it is a destiny thief. The Lord will avenge any insult you have received due to ingratitude.

Beloved, "the LORD will surely reward you with a lasting dynasty, for you are fighting the LORD's battles. And you have not done wrong throughout your entire life. Even when you are chased by those who seek to kill you, your life is safe in the care of the LORD your God, secure in his treasure pouch! But the lives of your enemies will disappear like stones shot from a sling!" (1 Samuel 25:28-29)

DEEP HUNGER IS PART OF THE DIVINE CODE

Many years ago, there was a crusade going on in Aalborg, Denmark. I had just completed my consulting assignment in Copenhagen and I knew in my spirit that I had to attend that crusade.

There were enough reasons for me to not attend, because the journey is just over five hours by train from Copenhagen to Aalborg. My assignment to the country was already complete, and staying longer would have incurred more accommodation costs. I could just get on a flight to London for the weekend to see my family or fly to Milan and relax with my aunt for less.

Besides, research showed me that the train from Copenhagen to Aalborg crosses a long bridge that would scare the mess out of someone afraid of heights. Also, I didn't even know anyone in Aalborg. I am not from Denmark. I had finished what I went there to do, and it was time to leave.

However, when you think you have it all figured out, God shows up and reminds you that you cannot talk your way out of it. He has his own assignment for you to complete in the region and you are not going to miss it.

When I got to church that weekend, I mentioned to someone that I was thinking of attending the crusade. Immediately, she picked up her phone, called a friend and her husband, and told them about me. They spoke to me and told me to come and stay with them in Aalborg, that they were attending the crusade too and we would go together.

Well, I received provision before even arriving at the destination. I could have talked myself out of the blessing that was attached to Aalborg especially reserved for me by God just by being complacent. He proved to me that I did not have to worry about anything. He provided free week-long accommodation plus easy access to the location without stress.

My new Danish friends welcomed me (did not know me, did not look like me in any way), did not speak English, prepared food for me like I was their long-lost sister, and shared a powerful testimony with me that

I will never forget. I got what I went to receive and it has been more fire ever since!

What was my excuse?
Nothing.
I had no excuse.
It was a mindset relapse.

A shift needed to take place. Just when you are about to talk yourself out of something, isn't it like God to place a destiny helper in your path who won't even necessarily look like you to stir up the gift in you or to jumpstart your faith so you do not miss what he has appointed for you?

When I got to the crusade, each day I received something. There was "fire," and I needed that fire to "burn" some things in my life. It was apparent that I needed to be there. I began moving with holy boldness, received divine visitations in a powerful dimension that I had never experienced before, gained some inexplicable clarity, and received divine directions that I have reserved for my speaking engagements.

HOW BADLY DO YOU WANT IT?

If you want something badly, you will go to great lengths to acquire it. Perhaps the Lord may just place a destiny helper in your path. Perhaps he may not. Regardless, if you stay in one position, you may just miss the blessing he has for you.

When you have a mental shift and decide to allow God to use you, he makes the resources available and the destiny helpers arise. Your assignment requires deep hunger for the things of God. You cannot be complacent or try to postpone its implementation. I have seen wonders work in my life and the lives of others, too, because of an elevated thirst for kingdom business, operations, and prosperity.

In the past, I would not reveal too much about my faith in the professional arena because I did not want people to act differently towards me or try to adjust themselves because I am an ordained pastor. However, I realized that it is imperative to be me in all circumstances, get hungry for God and use every opportunity for people to see the

Christ in me, the hope of glory.

I have also learned to just follow the leading of the Holy Spirit and trust God to take care of everything. In our obedience to God, he paves the way and awakens all the localized destiny helpers for the project. However, if we fail to act because we want things to be perfect, this is comparable to witchcraft. The Bible teaches us in 1 Samuel 15:22-23 (TLB) that "rebellion is as bad as the sin of witchcraft, and stubbornness is as bad as worshipping idols."

I have experienced the fire of the Holy Ghost and kick-started purposes so that destinies are fulfilled. I have first-hand knowledge and experience of the importance of deep hunger for God to successfully carry out his assignments. He even reveals barrier-breaking strategies in the midst of your quest for him.

Sometimes people perceive the Lord's assignment to be so huge and it involves many moving parts. However, your assignment may just be for you to write and publish your book. An interesting fact is that authors live twice through their books. When you are no longer on this earth, your book remains for generations to come.

Think about Charles Spurgeon. Charles Finney. These authors are from centuries ago, yet we still read their works and are blessed and motivated by them. No more excuses that you do not have money, you cannot write that book because you do not have time, you cannot travel because "there's a lion outside that might eat you" (Proverbs 22:13).

Whichever assignment the Lord has placed in your heart, may hunger for him never depart from you. Get up and go do what you must do. There is provision already assigned to the task. Didn't God assign ravens to feed Elijah at the Kerith Ravine? (1 Kings 17). If Elijah had remained where he was, what do you think would have happened to him?

CONSECRATION SETS THE TONE

Consecration involves the active role of setting yourself apart for the work the Lord has commanded you to carry out. You need to learn to leave some friends and family behind. It may sound selfish, but do you know that those people have their own destinies, and can interfere with yours?

If you continuously hang around people who do not understand your vision, at some point you will be discouraged and even freeze your purpose. At the end of the day, when God calls his children home, there is no group judgment day. Each person must account for his or her own life.

CONSECRATION IS NON-NEGOTIABLE

Set some time apart to seek the Lord's face before and during the implementation of your assignment. Remember, you are assigned to do great exploits and you need divine direction.

In my experience of planning and hosting apostolic events, I have since realized that without the help of God, they just will not succeed. There are many things that go into planning an event, and it even becomes tougher when you are assigned to territories where you do not know people.

In situations like that, I fasted and prayed to God to awaken destiny helpers in the region to come to our aid because I knew that their involvement would lighten the load. Besides, because God already assigned us, he would help to bring it to fruition.

There are many aspects involved in planning an event that brings all kinds of people together in one place, including selection of speakers, the ideal location, the event agenda, and the direction the Holy Spirit wants the event to go.

Consecration is imperative because as a leader, you are faced with decision-making. You deal with all kinds of spirits operating in different individuals. Some are for you and some are agents of the enemy sent to infiltrate your project.

WHEN YOU CONSECRATE YOURSELF, YOU SURRENDER TO GOD

Here I am, Lord. I give myself to you. You have assigned me to this territory. I don't know it very well but I trust in you to help me bring this vision you have given me to fruition. Without your help, I cannot do it. Dear Lord, soak me in your blood. Wash me clean so my conscience is clear. Help me, Lord, to stay focused, because I don't want to disappoint you.

The Bible teaches in Romans 12:1 (NIV) that "in view of God's mercy, to offer your bodies as a living sacrifice, holy and pleasing to God—this is your true and proper worship."

When we consecrate ourselves, we offer our bodies as a living sacrifice unto God. As part of giving our physical bodies to God, to carry out the assignment we must be careful about what goes in and touches our precious bodies. We need good health to do God's work.

Consecration presses for fasting and prayer. Part of setting our bodies as a living sacrifice unto God is to abstain from food for a specific period. In the operation of your assignment, you will encounter situations; some understandable, and some outright evil. In these situations, when your life is backed by prayer and fasting, you become unshakeable. Some situations cannot be dealt with unless by prayer and fasting.

TIME TO REFLECT

Are you doing anything now that can interfere with the state of your body and ability to carry out your assignment?

CONSECRATION PAYS OFF

Consecration is a strategy that paves the way for God to do the miraculous in our lives. Joshua told the people in Joshua 3:5: "Consecrate yourselves, for tomorrow the LORD will do amazing things among you."

Amazing things happen when we consecrate ourselves. It empowers us to prepare to receive the goodness of God. In the midst of consecration, holiness shows and is perceived by others. As much as holiness can make people feel uneasy, it can also open doors and bring about divine favor.

In 2 Kings 4:9-10, the woman in Shunem "perceived" Elisha to be a holy man of God. She gave him food at her place whenever he was in town, and even honored him by preparing a room for him. She said: "Let's build a small room for him on the roof and furnish it with a bed, a table, a chair, and a lamp. Then he will have a place to stay whenever he comes by."

As we carry out our assignments as the assigned, let us strive to be holy so we can walk in the totality of what God has ordained for us.

Four

YOUR ASSIGNMENT REQUIRES HOLY BOLDNESS

Sometimes your assignment is solo.

On your own.

Without the clique.

No saints or church folk.

The assigned are as bold as a lion. They operate with holy boldness and do not quit. It is said that eagles do not fly in flocks. Be prepared and fearless to do what you must do without the flock.

Are you an eagle? The eagle does not need "a convocation" or "flock," like geese, to soar. As you proceed and obey God, stop looking to be caged in a pen like chickens. One mistake often made is to wait for someone else to join us before we proceed with the assignment. The risk in this type of wait is that the enemy knows your weakness and can send a counterfeit; sometimes one you cannot refuse.

This *counterfeit* will supposedly complement you in the area where you lack confidence. How terrible it is for the person called by God to carry out an assignment with a counterfeit privy to inside information and determined to steal destinies!

If God wanted community activation for your assignment, he would have told you. It is imperative that you proceed with everything that is in you and do not inject a non-commissioned delay.

Back in the day when I started walking in my purpose, there were some things I really wanted to boldly carry out for God, but I delayed their implementation. I was surrounded by people who did not catch the vision and I allowed it to pitch a tent in my yard.

One day I realized that by failing to totally walk in what God had called me to do, I was operating in disobedience. I did not postpone the implementation because of fear. It was because I was looking at a "community project" when it was a "solo project."

As human beings, we have the tendency to operate like sheep. We do not move until one person moves and then everybody follows. What has God called you to do? Do you think he does not know your flaws? Do you think he does not know what you need?

In my situation, I desired the communal feeling of "this is what we are doing." Then I realized that if God wanted to involve others, he would have revealed the assignment to them.

This does not mean that you should reject help to carry out your projects. It means that you should fearlessly go and out and do whatever God has instructed you to do. He has helpers of destiny already waiting for you to take the first step.

APOSTLE PAUL WAS BOLD

Anytime I read the Acts of the Apostles, I am amazed at the boldness of the people God used mightily. Paul's love for Christ and the power that worked in him was simply unfathomable.

The Isle of Paphos
The enemy has a way of strategically positioning his agents in places (including high places and within government institutions). In Acts 13, Paul encountered a sorcerer in Paphos, a false prophet called Bar-Jesus who had attached himself to the governor, Sergius Paulus. This was

someone of considerable influence, a sagacious man.

He invited Saul and Barnabas to visit him. He wanted to hear the word of God. He gave them access to him. When we look at this, we see a great opportunity to minister about Jesus in high places. He was open to receiving them. He was interested.

However, someone evil had already attached himself to the governor. Bar-Jesus, Elymas—false prophet, sorcerer, wizard, demonic influence, bad spirit—also had the ear of the governor.

> But Elymas, the sorcerer (as his name means in Greek), interfered and urged the governor to pay no attention to what Barnabas and Saul said. He was trying to keep the governor from believing.
>
> Saul, also known as Paul, was filled with the Holy Spirit, and he looked the sorcerer in the eye. Then he said, "You son of the devil, full of every sort of deceit and fraud, and enemy of all that is good! Will you never stop perverting the true ways of the Lord?
>
> Watch now, for the Lord has laid his hand of punishment upon you, and you will be struck blind. You will not see the sunlight for some time." Instantly mist and darkness came over the man's eyes, and he began groping around begging for someone to take his hand and lead him.
>
> When the proconsul saw what had happened, he believed, for he was amazed at the teaching about the Lord.
>
> —Acts 13:8-12 (NLT)

In the spiritual realm, the battle was on. In your assignment, it is possible that you may encounter people who would have otherwise listened to you but for the interference of the devil's agents appointed to ruin your plans. Paul was bold; he told Elymas off and let him know what would happen to him for daring to interfere with the Lord's assignment.

In this amazing encounter at Paphos, we learn how to deal with the enemy. If you ever face something similar, remember what happened to Paul and Barnabas at Paphos. Operate with holy boldness, and tell that demonic force where to go.

Another important revelation at Paphos was that the distraction the enemy meant for evil, God turned around for good. The governor witnessed the destruction and downfall of Elymas the sorcerer; he believed and was amazed at the teaching about the Lord.

God will take out any evil force that dares to mess up your assignment. Your work will be accompanied by signs and wonders, just like Apostle Paul in Paphos. Any monitoring actions of the evil one will face mist and darkness and they shall see no more.

There is nothing new under the sun.

One reason why I have written this book is to show you that there is nothing new that has not happened before. In Acts 13, as Paul and Barnabas continued on their missionary journey teaching in synagogues and preaching to the Gentiles, the opposition did not stop. Jewish leaders did not like the crowds that followed them everywhere they went. They became jealous and slandered Paul, and argued against anything he said.

Social media today and the rise of the Internet has made it very easy for men and women of God to face defamation. Whatever you see today that affects the ministries of God's servants due to evil words and lies spread by agents of the devil is not new.

There are many public figures in ministry who have been lied about and stories cooked up to destroy their reputations because of jealousy. These miscreants of evil see a huge online following, large crowds of people following certain men and women of God; they become jealous, and argue against anything they say.

But *who are the people orchestrating the lies* and *why would they even do it*? There are a few reasons, but these are some of the most popular: religious spirits, traditionalism, and legalism.

As the assigned of God, remember, those who will believe, shall believe. Some will be stubborn, but do not allow their stubbornness to delay this assignment or the next.

Is that behavior new? No, it happened to Paul, too.

> But the Jewish leaders incited the God-fearing women of high standing and the leading men of the city. They stirred up persecution against Paul and Barnabas, and expelled them from their region.
>
> —Acts 13:50 (NIV)

But what did Paul and Barnabas do when faced with such persecution? Did they become stubborn and refuse to leave? No. Apparently, they shook the dust off their feet, left the people to their fate, and off they went on their next assignment: Iconium. They had done their job, and if the folks at Antioch refused to believe, it was not their fault.

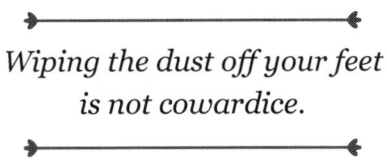

Wiping the dust off your feet is not cowardice.

THE ICONIUM EXPERIENCE

The rejection and slander Paul faced from enemies of progress did not stop the power of God to take place in Iconium. The Bible tells us that they preached with so much power that lots of Jews and Gentiles believed. In the midst of all that victory, there were still attacks to make people not believe the apostles. However, something happened that really caught my attention.

> But the apostles stayed there a long time, preaching boldly about the grace of the Lord. And the Lord proved their message was true by giving them power to do miraculous signs and wonders.
>
> —Acts 14:3 (NLT)

The assigned press forth to deliver notwithstanding opposition.

THE NEHEMIAH DELIVERANCE

Nehemiah faced opposition from people who were determined to see him fail at all costs. Have you ever been lied about? Have people falsely accused you because they wanted to take what you have, or just because the enemy infiltrated their minds and cooked up their thought process with evil?

God will show himself true in our obedience to the call. Just as he proved true the apostles' message by giving them power to do signs and wonders, he will do the same for you.

As you proceed with your assignment, think about these things:

- Can we have that kind of faith and determination in these times as we carry out our assignments?
- Can we proceed notwithstanding hatred, slander, floggings, and all types of strange manifestations?

THE HELPERS OF DESTINY

Five

YOUR ASSIGNMENT HAS COMPANIONS

Do you know that some people are assigned to you for the fulfillment of God's tasks? You cannot carry it out all by yourself. Allow people to help you, and apply discernment.

One trick of the enemy that interferes with the success of assignments is to make you think that the person or companion assigned to you is your enemy. This is easy to do. For example, when you are focused on destroying the devil, you may tag divine appointments as evil and evil appointments as divine.

It takes wisdom and the grace of God to decipher who is supposed to accompany or assist you and who you should avoid, but what is the big deal about these companions? Why should you care about them and who are they?

THE LEADER OF ANOTHER MINISTRY

It is not uncanny to have a man or woman totally committed to the fulfillment of the tasks God has given you. If you are the person God has called to assist another ministry, do not be afraid or think that all your own tasks will now be on the back burner.

Sometimes God will pull you from what you are doing to temporarily assist, mentor, or accompany another vessel. For example, when you look at the ministry of God's generals, sometimes you see they have worship leaders and other ministry leaders accompany them worldwide. It does not mean that they have abandoned their ministries or what God has called them to do. It just means that for that season, God requires their services elsewhere.

What about Apostle Paul in the Bible?

He was renowned for signs and wonders that accompanied his ministry, but he had John Mark accompany him and Barnabas on missions. Some people miss God's blessings because they want to be in the limelight instead of being in a role of servant leader.

This principle also applies to business.

When you consult for another corporation, it does not mean that you have abandoned your business. It just means that for a specific period or season, your gifts are transferred to another project, hopefully for the purpose of making the world a better place.

AN ANIMAL OR BIRD AS A COMPANION

There are times when your gifts will be borrowed for the effective delivery of another ministry's assignment. In the triumphant entry described in Matthew 21:1-11, the animals (donkey and colt) were not Jesus,' but were borrowed. They belonged to someone else, but the Master had need for them.

This was a fulfillment of what was already prophesied by Prophet Zechariah. Jesus rode on the donkey and colt, marching through Jerusalem.

In this situation, the colt, donkey, and disciples were Jesus' companions for the assignment in that city. As he went, the people ahead and behind him exclaimed:

"Hosanna to the Son of David!"

"Blessed is he who comes in the name of the Lord!"

"Hosanna in the highest."

Dear assigned, "the Master has need" of what you have. The Lord needs your gift. Yes, he does! Just as the colt and donkey were necessary for the fulfillment of prophecy, your gift is needed for the fulfillment of the assignment that has your name inscribed on it. Thank God that you have something valuable to someone else who desperately needs it for the Lord's glory and fulfillment of your predestined path!

AT ONE POINT, ELIJAH'S COMPANIONS WERE RAVENS

God can use whoever or whatever to accomplish his purpose. In the thick of things, when the word of the Lord came to Elijah to flee and hide in the Kerith Ravine, God sent ravens to feed him (1 Kings 17). As you proceed, God can use your companions to feed you so you will not be found wanting.

In this situation that Elijah found himself, his companions were the ravens assigned by God to assist him. The Lord surely knows how to provide for those whom he has called according to his purpose.

LESSONS FROM THE RAVENS

1. *Sometimes the role of your companion is to feed you.* God will assign a useful companion in any shape or form who will not be a burden but will help make your job easier. It is important to note that your obedience to God makes the role of your assigned companion easier; Elijah went to the exact place God told him to go to. He did not shillyshally. He did not go on a detour.

    Imagine if he had gone somewhere else; perhaps the expected provision by the ravens at the Kerith Ravine would not have occurred. It is possible that God's servant would have starved or be in more danger.

2. *When you are on God's assignment, do not focus on cosmetics.* Your companion may not look "clean" like you do. Elijah did not focus on the look or form of the companion, unclean birds. These are large, black birds that look like crows, with a wingspan of approximately fifty inches!

Ravens are not pet birds that children play with daily. Ravens are not parrots. These are scavengers that eat animals, plants, and sometimes mammals! Can you imagine eating bread and meat that a scavenger brings to you? I am sure many things would come to your mind, like: Where did they come from? Who sent them? Is it poisonous? Aren't they full of germs? Etc.

Whenever you hear the word raven, what comes to your mind?

I am reminded of the Scripture in Leviticus 11:13-19 (NLT) where God told Moses and Aaron to relay a message to the people of Israel about forbidden birds they must not eat.

> The griffon vulture, the bearded vulture, the black vulture, the kite, falcons of all kinds, ravens of all kinds, the eagle owl, the short-eared owl, the seagull, hawks of all kinds, the little owl, the cormorant, the great owl, the barn owl, the desert owl, the Egyptian vulture, the stork, herons of all kinds, the hoopoe, and the bat.

Why did God command a forbidden bird to bring food to his servant Elijah? Was it a test of his faith to see if he would eat the food? The Bible does not tell us the reason, but I must infer that there is always a purpose behind God's instruction. It is important for us to proceed with whatever he tells us to do, even if it does not make sense to us.

Did God go back on his word about the forbidden food? No, but he used what was forbidden to help his servant. Sometimes God's instrument of help might fall short of our own righteous standard.

3. *God will send you an intelligent companion for the assignment.* According to science, ravens are known to be intelligent birds. For example, they are great at hiding food, even from other ravens, and they usually get their food on the first try. It is possible that it is also because ravens know the territory. They are birds that fly and see what is on the ground and in the air.

Isn't it like God to choose purposeful companions to feed his servant Elijah? He made sure that his mode of transporting the food to Elijah would not fail, because ravens are smart birds!

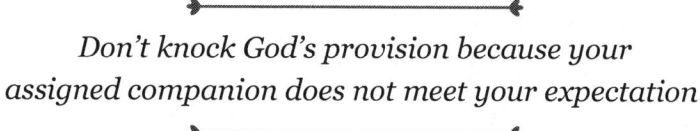

*Don't knock God's provision because your
assigned companion does not meet your expectation.*

Sometimes we reject help because we are accustomed to what "help" should look like. What is your own version of "raven" in your assignment journey? Who has God brought to you to "feed" you? Did you accept? Did you send him or her away?

Due to upbringing and exposure to certain prejudices, some people do not accept help from folks who do not look like, or talk like, them. This is because they think, "God just couldn't have sent him...He doesn't use people like that...Have you seen the number of tattoos on her body?"

This reminds me of the Scripture in Acts 10:10-15 (NIV) where Peter went up to the roof to pray and he was hungry.

> He became hungry and wanted something to eat, and while the meal was being prepared, he fell into a trance. He saw heaven opened and something like a large sheet being let down to earth by its four corners. It contained all kinds of four-footed animals, as well as reptiles and birds.
>
> Then a voice told him, "Get up, Peter. Kill and eat." "Surely

not, Lord!" Peter replied. "I have never eaten anything impure or unclean." The voice spoke to him a second time, "Do not call anything impure that God has made clean."

Peter, God's servant, called what he saw unclean and he was scolded by God. On your assignment, remember to not call whatever God has made clean as unclean. It may not look like our expectation, but God knows best.

THE TALKING DONKEY

In Numbers 22, we read that Balaam started off on a mission to go and meet Balak, the king of Moab, who had a very strange request. Balaam was instructed by God to only speak whatever he told him. We also read that God was not happy with Balaam because he went. Hence, God assigned an angel to block Balaam.

In Balaam's situation, his companion was a donkey whom the Lord later made to speak. This donkey protected Balaam when the angel of the Lord could have taken him out. He stopped moving when he should have kept going.

> Balaam's donkey saw the angel of the LORD standing in the road with a drawn sword in his hand. The donkey bolted off the road into a field, but Balaam beat it and turned it back onto the road.
>
> Then the angel of the LORD stood at a place where the road narrowed between two vineyard walls. 25 When the donkey saw the angel of the LORD, it tried to squeeze by and crushed Balaam's foot against the wall. So Balaam beat the donkey again.
>
> —Numbers 22:23-25 (NLT)

Balaam struck his donkey multiple times because he did not like its behavior. He was angry. Do you know that your companion may just be with you for your own protection? If he, she, or it starts to act strangely, perhaps the best thing to do is to find out why rather than attempt to destroy it.

DESTINY NOTE

*Do not send people away God has appointed to you because they do not look like your expectation.
They may halt their help in the middle of your journey and it can be for a reason that protects your destiny.
God can use anybody and anything to get his message across.*

THE 12 DISCIPLES (COMPANIONS) AND JESUS' MINISTRY

While on earth, Jesus Christ had twelve disciples. They accompanied him. They ate with him. They learned from him. They observed what he did. They saw one miracle after another. They left whatever they were doing to follow him. Jesus Christ had companions.

Even though Christ declared on the cross, "It is finished," his assignment created more followers across the earth and is still growing today. A finished assignment isn't necessarily the end, but a conduit for salvation. Christ declared on the cross, "It is finished," but his assignment makes us live.

His assignment gives us faith, hope, and love.

His assignment makes us whole.

His assignment brings emancipation.

Now we are his companions, "friends of God," "gods" (Psalm 82:6) and really, believers carrying out his tasks for the purpose of replication and salvation. The completion of the assignment was just the beginning of something new.

Later, knowing that everything had now been finished, and so that Scripture would be fulfilled, Jesus said, "I am thirsty." A jar of wine vinegar was there, so they soaked a sponge in it, put the sponge on a stalk of the hyssop plant, and lifted it to Jesus' lips. When he had received the drink, Jesus said, "It is finished." With that, he bowed his head and gave up his spirit.

—John 19:28-30 (NIV)

Six

YOUR ASSIGNMENT HAS A MENTOR

I like to define the meaning of *mentor* as "someone appointed to help you go through a training process smoothly."

Not too long ago, I started a mentorship program for women in ministry and business. I realized that many people need help, and because God has blessed me with gifts, talents, knowledge, and skills, it would be a disservice to the community to hoard them and not teach people how to fish.

During the program, confidential sharing and releasing was involved. I learned a lot too about the power of communication and the ability to think swiftly on one's feet. Mentoring is great, but a real learning process.

Sometimes we fail to help people because we think what we know will not help them, they won't listen, or if they listen, they won't apply it. How about you just help someone and let the seed fall wherever it may?

When I first started out in ministry, I searched for women who were like me and doing what the Lord had called them to do. Some were approachable, some were not, due to strange protocols.

One day I had a conversation with a pastor about ministry, and he said that most female senior pastors he knew were either widows, divorced, or never married. What he said did not sit well with me. He did not say it to discourage me, but he just said that it was the people he knew. He agreed that women should be in ministry because Galatians 3:28 says, "There is neither Jew or Gentile, neither slave or free, nor is there male and female, for you are all one in Christ Jesus."

The encounter made me do some research, and I found renowned women in leadership roles in ministries; many are senior pastors of thriving churches today. They are married.

Now, back to my reason for saying that your assignment requires a mentor. You need to be aligned with someone who understands the call of God upon your life. That particular discussion happened when I was searching for a mentor to guide me. The conversation was with a powerful man of God, but if I did not know myself, I would have been discouraged. Maybe you wouldn't even be reading this book today.

If I had allowed other people's views or thinking to influence mine or the call of God upon my life, perhaps none of our ministries would have been launched or be in full operational mode.

DO YOU HAVE A MENTOR?

If you don't have one, I pray the Lord shows you the assigned one. Remember that your mentors should be accessible and should tell you the truth; not be condescending, but real in all ways.

But, how do you approach the mentor?

Send an email or find out the best mode of contact and reach out. Ask him or her. Go straight to the point and tell them why you think it would be a good fit. When you find the right mentor you will know, because he or she will carry a special anointing to solve a particular problem you may have or your audience has.

The blessing of mentorship is that you greatly cut the time you spend trying to figure things out on your own. During my mentorship program, things became clear for my mentees; they received clarity and were empowered to do great exploits.

DON'T UNDERESTIMATE THE POWER OF MENTORSHIP

Didn't Jesus mentor his twelve disciples? Many times. In the Bible we see him coaching and telling them what to do. He was with Peter on the boat in Luke 5 and Peter toiled day and night but could not catch fish. Then Jesus Christ told him what to do. What happened next was that he caught a great number of fish and he needed help from other fishermen to continue.

A mentor can help you solve a particular problem and end fruitless labor.

A MENTOR CAN ALSO BE A DESTINY HELPER

He or she may have connections that can take you to your next level. In the Bible, Paul talked about Phoebe. We do not know much about her, but he spoke highly of her as a helper of destiny; a deacon in the church.

> I commend to you Phoebe our sister, who is a servant of the church in Cenchreae, that you may receive her in the Lord in a manner worthy of the saints, and assist her in whatever business she has need of you; for indeed she has been a helper of many and of myself also.
>
> —Romans 16:1-2 (New King James Version)

YOUR MENTOR CAN BE YOUNGER THAN YOU

Expect it. Age has nothing to do with it. Didn't Daniel help the mighty Nebuchadnezzar? What has the Wisdom of Solomon got to do with the age of Methuselah? Nothing. Sometimes, we fail to accept help because of legalism or religion. What is important is the knowledge, skills, and anointing that he or she carries to help you implement what you need to do smoothly.

What about *Priscilla* and *Aquila*? Didn't they mentor Apollos in Acts 18? They saw that his ministry was filled with eloquence and he boldly taught about the baptism of John but needed to know more.

Didn't Apostle Paul mentor many? He was the same guy formerly called Saul who terrorized and killed people in his before-Christ days. I love his mentoring principle that is based on 1 Corinthians 11:1 (Amplified Bible): "Imitate me, just as I imitate Christ."

If you have a mentor, how is he or she leading? Does he or she follow Christ, so you can follow Christ and teach others too to follow Christ? Is he or she a toxic mentor with a controlling spirit? Remember that your reason for seeking a mentor in the first place is because you need strategic help, not someone who will put you in bondage!

What about you? Are you currently a mentor? The power of mentorship is that it creates ripple effects. Each one, reach one; it continues and spreads like wildfire. Are you reaching one, and is the one you are reaching also reaching another?

Have you identified whom the Lord has assigned to help you on this journey? This is your destiny helper.

Seven

YOUR ASSIGNMENT HAS ORDAINED TIMING

YOU ARE EXPECTED TO UNDERSTAND THE TIMES

There is a time to be known and a time to hide; not because you are foolish or a coward, but because you understand the times and you move as led by the Holy Spirit.

Your silence can be misconstrued for weakness or cowardice but those who are led by the Spirit of God are children of God (Romans 8:14), and God certainly takes care of his assigned seed! Do not bite any bait and be forced to enter into any hasty collaboration.

If you do not understand the times, three things can happen.

1. The enemy can easily trap you.
2. You can halt your destiny by entering an agreement God did not ordain.
3. Nonchalance or lack of awareness of the times can hinder blessings of your seed and future generations.

This is one reason why we must pray for the "Issachar anointing"—for God to help us understand the times that we are in, when to move or when to stay, whether to speak or whether to stay silent, to fight or to wait.

In 1 Chronicles 12:32, the men of Issachar understood the signs of the times and knew the best course for Israel to take. Your destiny is too important to step out when you should sit down. Your life is too precious to fly when you should walk. Your purpose is too significant to crawl when you should run.

Many mistakes in life can be avoided and averted if we understand the times that we are in and not allow frustration to push us to hasty decisions.

Desperation can make you misunderstand the times.

In desperate times, because you really want something badly, you may just proceed with what you should wait for, and even convince yourself that you are doing the right thing.

Get wisdom and direction from the word of God and yield to the voice of the Holy Spirit; that still, small voice that we don't want to hear sometimes. As you yield to understand the times, ponder the path of your feet and know that sometimes, the enemy will lure you to enticing destinations to trap you.

However, you remain steadfast in your belief, knowing that God will not allow your feet to stumble because you are in tune with the Holy Spirit. Every evil appointment arranged to derail your destiny is destroyed in Jesus' name.

GOD CAN HIDE YOU FOR A REASON

Sometimes God will hide you for your own safety, especially because he loves you so much and does not want anything bad to happen to you.

In your season of hiding, sometimes everything you expect to work in your life just won't work.

When you are in the hiding place, it may not be fun because everyone you know is out there in the limelight, seemingly enjoying abundant life, and it appears that you are not.

Trust God's timing.
He hid Moses for a reason.
He hid Elijah at the Kerith Brook.
He hid Jonah in the whale's belly for a reason.

Oftentimes, God will hide you because he knows what is ahead. Ever been in a situation where no matter what you try to do to get to a certain place (even if all the finances and support are in order), somehow you are unable to go?

I heard a story about someone who was supposed to go on a mission trip but fell ill. He had all the finances together, had already set the date and bought the plane ticket, but fell seriously ill. The enemy brought a dreadful diagnosis but due to divine intervention and heavenly interception, he got a clean bill of health.

The best part of the story was that in that period of abandoned journey, he was able to minister to and pray for some people. He did not feel disappointed that he did not go on the trip because it could have been worse. What if the sickness appeared when he was out of the country, away from his doctor and excellent medical facilities?

God knew what was ahead and cancelled the trip for him. In his temporary period of hiding, he learned a lot about himself and took the focus off himself to pray for others.

Isn't it like God to change our plans for his plans? Proverbs 19:21 teaches us that we can make many plans, but the Lord's purpose shall prevail.

Sometimes your hiding can be a result of God using someone else to tell you to flee for your safety so that your destiny will not be aborted. Esau planned to kill Jacob, but when their mother heard about it (Genesis 27:41-45), she told Jacob to flee to their uncle Laban until his brother had cooled down (at least).

An angel told Joseph to flee with Mary and baby Jesus (Matthew

2:13) because of the spirit of Herod in operation—to abort the destinies of male children (kill them) under two years old.

A TIME OF DESTINY INCUBATION

In your season of divine hiding, God places you in what I call a destiny incubator to protect and prepare you for the outside world. When babies are born prematurely, to save them and to care for them properly because they are not ready for the world of germs and microbes, they are placed in incubators.

A baby who leaves his mother's womb prematurely usually does not have fully formed organs, such as lungs, and needs help to thrive. Hence, the reason for incubators. They protect babies from infection, keep them warm, and protect them from environmental allergens.

In your destiny walk, the *destiny incubator* is the place of divine protection for your development and preservation. Sometimes we launch prematurely and if not for the grace of God, terrible things could have happened.

God loves you so much that he places his people in destiny incubators. Some call destiny incubators "divine wilderness" or dry season. An example of how you are placed in a destiny incubator is that you experience a season of inexplicable drought and nothing you do works.

Perhaps the Lord wants to prepare you for his assignment and in the incubator, you are shifted from an atmosphere of noise, friends, and foe, and protected for your own good. Sometimes your most trusted friends will even vanish.

However, regardless of the circumstance, for some folks, it is in the *destiny incubator* that healing takes place. Formation occurs. Then they are released to launch because they are ready.

If you find yourself suddenly placed in a destiny incubator, like the Lord did to Jonah in the belly of the whale, understand that it is for your own good. You matter. Your assignment matters, and a premature delivery of what you are supposed to carry out will not have the desired impact.

In my walk, I have seen that the swiftness of your deliverance can depend on how you see the unpleasant situation and how badly you want change. I have also seen that the release of your blessing depends on your faith and what you believe.

The indignation will surely pass because God has already set a time for you to come out and be known. He spoke to Moses (Exodus 3:1-12) when he was tending his father-in-law's flock. Remember that Moses was already away from his people, and it was now time for him to start to walk in his assignment.

Don't launch into the deep before its ordained timing. You may not like the timing but hold onto this Word:

> Come, my people, enter your chambers, and shut your doors behind you; hide yourself, as it were, for a little moment, until the indignation is past.
>
> —Isaiah 26:20

THE KINGDOM EXPECTATIONS

YOUR ASSIGNMENT REQUIRES A DEFINED PLATFORM

Some people seek platforms because they want to be noticed, and stubbornly refuse to activate their God-ordained "platform builder" roles. If God has already instructed you to build platforms, why are you pursuing (and even begging) others to give you a platform (that is most likely not designed for your destiny)?

Why cry, "God, open doors, give me a bus," when God has already shown you an airplane? Sometimes, because we want to be like others, we try to build 1,000,000 when God's instruction is 100.

YOU CANNOT BORROW ANOTHER PERSON'S ASSIGNMENT

God knows why he chose you to do what you are created to do, and he knows why he chose that person to do whatever he or she is doing. If God has called you to the marketplace, thrive and make an impact on that platform. If your assignment is to teach the Word weekly from the pulpit within a church building, then do it with love, grace, fire, and power.

Focus on God's number, not human numbers, and stay in your lane.

Sometimes, because we don't want to rock the boat, we focus on building 100 when God has already shown us 1,000,000. With human wisdom, it takes too much work, effort, and money to build a multitude. The safe place of 100 is easier. What an error!

If you boldly profess that Elohim is your God, the One who specializes in impossible cases, you will proceed against all odds. He chose you, right? Then, he will provide; but you can't be disobedient and roll with 100, when there are 999,900 waiting for you to bring forth what God has reserved for them.

Understand the "ministry" that God has placed in your hands.

- Is it to reach the unsaved? Is it to teach the saved? Is it to show God's children how to use their gifts and talents? Is it to heal the sick? Is it to build the church? Is it to be you in the marketplace and still win souls for the kingdom?
- Is it to use your craftsmanship for the betterment of the church?

> Bezalel (Exodus 31:1-6) wasn't a preacher but he was an excellent craftsman, anointed to design and construct the Lord's tabernacle.

WHAT IS YOUR ASSIGNMENT AND TO WHOM?

What is your platform? Today, spend some time and really think about it. The called are assigned projects by God with allocated audiences. You are not called for nothing. Your assignment carries weight, and some folks in your camp will not have the kind of faith you possess to implement it.

THE ASSIGNMENT COMES WITH A CUSTOMIZED MANTLE

Many problems arise when we take on roles that God did not design for our destinies. When you read about David in 1 Samuel 17:38-39 (AMP), he rejected King Saul's garment and armor to fight Goliath. He did not wear them because he was not used to them.

> Then Saul dressed David in his garments and put a bronze helmet on his head, and put a coat of mail (armor) on him. Then David fastened his sword over his armor and tried to walk, [but he could not,] because he was not used to them. And David said to Saul, "I cannot go with these, because I am not used to them." So David took them off.

You are already equipped to carry out certain tasks given to you by God. In fact, because of your uniqueness, you are the only one who can carry them out.

Let's imagine that David actually wore the king's royal war garments, including boots that were not designed for his feet size. What do you think would have happened to the situation with Goliath?

In my opinion, it would have been a situation where he looked prepared for war on the outside but was really unprepared within. Remember, Goliath was prepared. He came to David with a spear and javelin, and he knew that he was strong.

However, the strength of Goliath could not match the gift, confidence, and courage of David that was backed by the power of Almighty God, Elohim. David told him in verse 45-46:

> You come to me with a sword, a spear, and a javelin, but I come to you in the name of the LORD of hosts, the God of the armies of Israel, whom you have taunted. This day the LORD will hand you over to me, and I will strike you down and cut off your head.

To implement your assignment successfully with impact, walk in your own customized outfit. You have what it takes to do it well.

THE CUSTOMIZED MANTLE REQUIRES PASSION

Your *assignment* is not a to-do list. It is more than that. Schoolchildren and college students face consequences if they fail do their assignments. As the assigned, there are consequences for disobedience too.

However, when it comes to an assignment given by God, it must be carried out diligently, whether we like it or not. To be successful, it must be carried out with passion for the things of God.

As human beings, our attention span is short, and people tune out if the assigned talks nonchalantly about Jesus and without enthusiasm. The Gospel of Jesus Christ is good news. How do you deliver good news to someone about, for example, he or she has won a million dollars? Do you frown, have a scowl on your face when you are happy, or do you smile and share with excitement?

Sometimes when we have a to-do list, we become anxious and concerned that we will not be able to complete all the tasks. In some situations, we freeze, and just give up. In other situations, we do whatever we can and deal with the consequences later.

*If you operate your assignment as a to-do list,
you may become agitated and frustrated.*

When you move with the Holy Spirit, there is no timer. We cannot place a time limit or schedule on the things of God. The best thing is to flow with whatever the Holy Spirit says and *learn to listen*. Do not allow frustration to make you miss the instruction or direction.

DIVINE DIRECTION IS REQUIRED

This is so important because many people have embarked on journeys God did not send them. People receive trouble when they go on assignments based on the flesh instead of assignments based on the promise of God or due to his divine mandate.

Do you know that if you do what God did not tell you to do, you may just succeed at it in the eyes of men, but it could be failure in the Lord's sight? After all, he has given us free will, right? In my walk, I often say, "Lord, if this is not of you, please do not make it happen. Don't let me go on an assignment you did not ordain for me. I want to fulfill my destiny, Lord. Thank you."

A simple prayer like that can prevent you from man-made obstacles. These are the types of obstacles that arise because of disobedience to God or reliability on human thinking, feelings, or imaginations.

In ministry, I have seen folks who start churches when God did not directly tell them to. Some are pastors because the title sounds good, yet they do not walk in the position. Some embark on journeys because a certain man or woman of God or prophet told them that he or she has seen a vision.

What did God tell you?

There is a difference between the called and those who just went. When God calls you to do something, he makes a way for it to be done. He equips you for the role, even if you think you do not qualify.

Wasn't David minding the sheep when he was called? Sometimes God may even use one of his servants, men or women, to appoint you to carry out his tasks. Discernment is heavily recommended so you do not fall into the hands of enemies of progress who desire to build empires and not God's kingdom.

The question then arises, who, should you listen to or believe that he or she is really sent by the Lord to you?

PAY ATTENTION TO THE TRACK RECORD OF THE MESSENGER

Look at David's life in the Bible. It was Samuel the prophet who anointed him, but who gave Samuel the authority to do it? Samuel did not spring up overnight. He had history. People knew him. He was not a *fly-by-night prophet*. The Bible teaches us in 1 Samuel 3:20:

And all Israel from Dan [in the north] to Beersheba [in the south] knew that Samuel was appointed as a prophet of the LORD.

HAVE YOU SEEN THEIR FRUITS?

The Bible tells us that by their fruits we shall know them. What have you heard about the messenger that is saying: "God sent me to you?"

If you embark on a misdirected journey, it will not only affect your destiny but the lives of all the people that are attached to your purpose. Therefore, divine direction is extremely important in the fulfillment of your destiny and all assignments that you need to carry out.

Nine

YOUR ASSIGNMENT REQUIRES REVELATION

The assignment that the Lord has entrusted into your hands requires a complete revelation of the Lord Jesus Christ. Do you remember Apollos? Acts 18:24-26 in the Bible tells us that:

> Meanwhile, a Jew named Apollos, an eloquent speaker who knew the Scriptures well, had arrived in Ephesus from Alexandria in Egypt. He had been taught the way of the Lord, and he taught others about Jesus with an enthusiastic spirit and with accuracy. However, he knew only about John's baptism. When Priscilla and Aquila heard him preaching boldly in the synagogue, they took him aside and explained the way of God even more accurately.

Apollos was fluent, bold, and spoke powerfully in public. He knew the Word, but he did not have the complete picture. He needed to know about the ministry of Jesus Christ so that the total emancipation of people would occur. He knew about John's baptism, which was about repentance and to prepare for the coming of the Lord.

Apollos had a great oratorical gift but for his assignment to make greater impact, he needed something else. I enjoyed reading about him because he had a teachable spirit. His story is a lesson for all of us on our journeys. Let us not think that we know too much and cannot be taught more for the proper implementation of our assignments.

Thank God for leaders who can see the gift in you and pull you aside without condemnation or superiority and teach and encourage you. Priscilla and Aquila did it. They explained the way of the Lord more to Apollos.

I have seen preachers act rudely to other preachers they deemed did not have "power." I have heard:

He is eloquent, but no power.
She is eloquent, but no power.
He has power, but too much theatrics.
He is anointed, but can't speak "proper English."
Nobody ever falls down when he lays hands on people.
Her preaching is too soft and makes people sleep.
His preaching is too high-energy for me.
He does not preach salvation, only "feel good" messages.
She only preaches about prosperity.

CAN YOU BELIEVE THAT CRITICISM IS HAPPENING IN THE BODY OF CHRIST?

When will it end? When will people wake up and understand that it is about Jesus and not them? God gives gifts to his children and assigns them to specific territories where those gifts will be used effectively. If you are eloquent, roll with it and be yourself. Do not water down who you are because some folks have nothing to do but talk all day!

Imagine if you are in the midst of Bible scholars who unfailingly nitpick every word another preacher speaks or writes. If you are not eloquent, and are unsure of what you are saying, your actions will confirm their preconceived doubts about you.

Now, remember the Bible does not say that what Apollos was doing was wrong. It is just that it was not the complete story. Apollos' gift made room for him during the implementation of his assignment.

> He proved to be of great benefit to those who, by God's grace, had believed. He refuted the Jews with powerful arguments in public debate.
>
> —Acts 18:27-28 (NLT)

He debated people who did not believe that the Messiah had come. Was Apollos' eloquence not right after all? He was bold. He spoke up. He talked. When you add eloquence to fire or power, something great happens.

As believers, we are to encourage each other and not tear each other down. A great example was when Apollos wanted to go to Achaia. The brothers and sisters in Ephesus encouraged him, and even wrote to the believers in Achaia to welcome him. Can that happen today? Will other men and women of God write to other leaders in the city you are going to carry out an assignment to welcome you? Some will do that. Others may not.

There seems to be a huge competition going on in the Church that needs to stop. When the focus is taken off Jesus Christ and placed on self-recognition and possession, people miss the point—and those who are supposed to receive salvation miss it too!

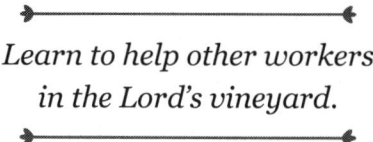

Learn to help other workers in the Lord's vineyard.

If you or someone you know is going on an assignment in, for example, Japan, and you know people there who can be beneficial to the assignment, do not wait to be asked. Offer your help to him or her and contact the people you know to receive the servant of God.

As the assigned you are a change agent, and a shift must take place. Make things happen. Make impact. Stagnation is not your portion. Fear is not your portion. Misery is not your portion. Frustration is not your portion. Confusion is not your portion.

Your portion is clarity, implementation, and completion.

Ten

LET THE WORK BE AUTHORIZED

Obedience to God is more important than "religious talk," and authorized kingdom work is better than popularity. Why?

- Because you can sound religious and still miss heaven.
- Because you can be successful in disobedience.
- Because it is only those who do the will of God in heaven that will pass through the gates.

Why is this important?

> Knowing the correct password—saying "Master, Master," for instance—isn't going to get you anywhere with me. What is required is serious obedience—doing what my Father wills. I can see it now—at the Final Judgment thousands strutting up to me and saying, "Master, we preached the Message, we bashed the demons, our God-sponsored projects had everyone talking."

> And do you know what I am going to say? "You missed the boat. All you did was use me to make yourselves important. You don't

impress me one bit. You're out of here."

—Matthew 7:21-23 (The Message)

It is a disservice to those who we are assigned to lead into freedom to carry out work that is not authorized by God. Just as we desire to walk in the will of God, they too desire the same thing and do not want to be led astray in any way.

When we obey God in totality, it is "like a person building a house who digs deep and lays the foundation on solid rock. When the floodwaters rise and break against that house, it stands firm because it is well built" (Luke 6:46 NLT).

What is the guarantee that the work you "purportedly" do in the Lord's name will last? What happens if he did not send you? What happens when he sends you?

WHAT IS UNAUTHORIZED WORK FOR CHRIST?

1. Borrowing and implementing someone else's purpose.
2. Starting a church and being the shepherd when God did not anoint you for it.
3. Preaching in the streets when you should be in the palace.
4. Preaching in the palace when you should be in the streets.
5. Conference-hopping all in the name of "working for Christ" and speaking church lingo.
6. Failure to launch exactly what God tells you to do.

An "unauthorized work for Christ" is doing something that God did not ask you to do. One mistake I have seen in ministry is that pastors try to be everything to everybody. Hence, there are many dying in the pews within the house of God. Let us strive only to do whatever God tells us to do.

Eleven

YOUR ASSIGNMENT REQUIRES EDUCATION

Do you know that your assignment requires education? I don't mean formal education (although that is beneficial). I am talking about educating yourself about certain practices, the culture, and people of your assignment territory.

Many years ago, I read a book by a highly sought-after man of God whom I respected and followed. Then I came across a page in one of his books where he referred to Africans as savages. I was upset because I could not understand why this person who preached around the world would call Africans "savages."

A savage is someone who is meant to be wild, unrestrained, uncontrolled, and of animalistic behavior.

THAT DID IT FOR ME

My faith was already rooted in Christ Jesus, but his preaching and teaching turned me off. I was no longer interested in whatever he had to say.

Aren't all of us one in Christ regardless of color?

What if I wasn't a believer already and I saw that? In my eyes, his evangelistic mission was already moot. Over the years, did his view change? I do not know. Perhaps it is really true that you can't teach an old dog new tricks. It is between him and the Lord. We do not judge. God is the One who will take care of it.

On another occasion, a preacher posted on social media that he was on his way to "the dark continent." I wanted to know why Africa was dubbed the Dark Continent. Was it because of race? Was it because of the slave trade? Who coined that phrase? Why would a preacher think he was on his way to save Africans? In fact, many African men and women are being used mightily by God to transform lives across the world (including outside the African continent).

I HAD MANY QUESTIONS

I know there are many beliefs that are certainly not Christian, and people need Jesus, but these practices are in other continents too. Evil is evil in any part of the world. Witchcraft is witchcraft whether in Asia, America, Europe, or Africa. Many people worship other gods and engage in evil practices in different continents.

It made me do online research about the supposedly "Dark Continent" and I was appalled by what I found. It is pretty clear that preconceived perceptions can hinder missions and even halt destinies, so we must educate ourselves.

How do you see others who do not look or talk like you?

As the assigned by God to carry out projects, we must educate ourselves and know what is happening; what is cool and what is not cool anymore. It is a new era, and times have not necessarily changed but are changing. The only thing that is unbroken and does not change is the word of God.

I do believe that if you really want to know about Africa (to explore or to preach), go directly to the source—ask an African. If you desire to go to a country within the continent of Africa to preach the gospel of

Jesus Christ, understand the culture, learn some things, and do not use offensive, archaic words that will render your mission moot.

The Bible says that we should not become a stumbling block (1 Corinthians 10:32). Let it not be said that it is your behavior that drove people away; those who initially wanted to know more about Jesus Christ.

Cultural education is very important, especially if your assignment is to win souls for the kingdom of God. People connect with you more when you show that you have at least made an effort to understand them and even tried to connect with them.

Twelve

FRUITFULNESS IS NON-NEGOTIABLE

We have a mandate in Genesis 1 to be fruitful and to multiply. Your assignment is expected to bear fruit. Fruitfulness is not always about financial prosperity.

Fruitfulness can be the ability to fulfill a need at very short notice.

Fruitfulness can also be the case of one planting the seed and the other watering. Each person has his or her own assignment, and fruitfulness will occur in varied ways. The ability to bear fruit can occur based on the completion of your assignment.

In 1 Corinthians 3:6-7, Paul said he *planted* and Apollos *watered*. Some may think that fruitfulness did not happen because the one who planted did not bring the increase. His assignment in that situation was to plant.

Apollos' assignment was to water. Was it fruitful? Yes, the seed was sown and what it needed to grow was the water and that was taken care of.

Problems occur when the one who is assigned to water decides to plant and the one assigned to plant starts to water. When the expected result does not happen, people start talking and pointing fingers.

Paul also mentioned that what is important is God, because he is the One who gives the increase. Regardless of the issue we place before us as the assigned, we must remember that the glory belongs to God and he decides how the dice falls.

SOME REASONS FOR FRUITLESS ASSIGNMENTS

WE LAUNCH OUT INTO THE DEEP WHEN WE SHOULD JUST WAIT

Do you know that your assignment could just be to conceive an idea and share it with another vessel ordained to implement it? Just because you have an idea does not mean you should be the one to implement it. Inception is different from strategy. Identify your position and stick with it.

WE SURROUND OURSELVES WITH FOLKS WITHOUT INSIGHT OR VISION

One reason it appears that your situation has been non-progressive for a long time is because of your close connections, your inner circle members. They cannot see beyond their locale. How do you carry out a global vision when your closest allies and confidantes only believe in thinking small?

Do you want to be fruitful in your assignment? Then, always remember that the world is your oyster. It is not easy to crack open but when you do, you will discover amazing treasures waiting to be discovered.

You know the vision the Lord has given you and the assignment he placed in your heart. Seek clarity from the Holy Spirit. It is imperative that you listen attentively and not allow folks with ulterior motives to rephrase the message and misdirect the assignment.

REFLECTIONS

Since you started your assignment, have you borne fruit? What are the results? Souls saved? Lives transformed? Destinies launched? Purposes activated? Abundant living?

As you carry out your assignment, do it with all your heart because it is expected that it will produce fruit. God will not send you on a futile assignment because he loves his children so much.

If things look withered, then it is time to reflect and uproot the cause of the inability to bear fruit. Hopelessness is not part of your assignment, and if it has attached itself in any way, it is time to uproot it and make sure it never returns.

To be fruitful in our assignments, we must remain connected to the Source and Provider of all things. Jesus is the vine and we are the branches (John 15). He instructs that if we remain in him and his words remain in us; that is, if we are deeply connected to him and whatever he says lives in our hearts, then whatever we ask for we shall receive.

The reality is that branches receive nutrients from the vine. The branch survives based on what it receives from the vine. In other words, the kind of fruitfulness we seek can only be found when we are connected to Christ.

As the branch on Christ the Vine, is your connection to the Vine secure enough to produce fruit in your assignment? Is there anything blocking you from receiving nourishment from Christ to be fruitful in your tasks?

YOU ARE NOT A ONE-TIME FRUIT BEARER

God did not create us to be one-time fruit bearers. The Scripture teaches us that "every branch that continues to bear fruit, He [repeatedly] prunes, so that it will bear more fruit [even richer and finer fruit]" (John 15:1-2).

If you are a gardener or farmer, you prune dead or withered parts because you do not want what you have invested in to be destroyed. You cut off growth-blockers because your investment has the capacity to grow. It can bear fruit and you want it to look its best. You want it to produce the best.

You are God's investment. He wants you to bear fruit, and that is why he has cut off dead things around you. When you bear fruit, he helps you to continue to bear more fruit. You are expected to bear fruit that remains, and that means, notwithstanding circumstances, we must remain in Christ and continue to bear fruit.

Even if strong and strange winds blow that try to interfere with our fruit-bearing process, we continue to produce. We do not give up. We do not wait to be cut off. We persist with the belief that because we are attached to the Vine, our efforts will not be fruitless.

Sometimes the enemy will attack to make you give up on what you are supposed to do. Even if you are at the lowest point in your life, you must push to bear fruit. You are already authorized by God to produce (multiply).

REMEMBER, YOU ARE NOT ALONE

He who has appointed you to carry out the assignment will ensure that you receive the nourishment you need to keep going. However, you must proceed. God has "appointed and placed and purposefully planted you" (John 15:16) to make things happen.

FRUITLESSNESS HAS CONSEQUENCES

We cannot just pretend to bear fruit, because fruitlessness has consequences regardless of who you are. The Bible teaches us in John 15:2 that "Every branch in Me that does not bear fruit, He takes away." One thing the Lord will not do is compel you to do your assignment. You must own your free will and exercise it.

The Lord expects to see our fruits.

"As Jesus was returning to the city, he was hungry. He saw a fig tree along the road, but when he came to it, he found nothing except leaves. Then he said to it, "You'll never again bear fruit!" The fig tree dried up at once" (Matthew 21:18-22).

Understand how fig trees bear fruit. They usually produce fruit before the leaves show. However, in this case, it had leaves but no fruit. It had the appearance of fruitfulness but bore no fruit.

IN OUR LIVES AND WALK WITH CHRIST, DO WE FEIGN FRUITFULNESS?

People see you on social media as fruitful but in reality there is no impact, no spiritual fruitfulness. We know not the hour or time the Master comes but if he comes today, will he find you fruitless? Think about it.

LET'S MAKE THINGS HAPPEN

Thirteen

YOUR ASSIGNMENT NEEDS THE OUTSTRETCHED HAND OF GOD

When the hand of God touches you, things shift. Barriers break. Gates are flung wide open. The sea parts for you to cross. As the assigned, we need the hand of God to touch our every move and the many lives we meet.

Why do we need God's outstretched hand?

The reality is that God is the One who holds our breath in his hand and owns all our ways (Daniel 5:23). When you know that your life is in his hands, the very breath that we breathe is up to him, we definitely need his hands to grab us and never let us go!

On our assignment journey, it is imperative that we consistently pray for God to keep us in the palm of his hands. I have experienced situations where if it was not for God, nothing we did would have worked. If it was up to us, we would have gone on assignments based on human desire and not what the Lord ordained. We would have listened to human beings in the form of "preachers" who had ulterior motives instead of adhering to the voice of the Holy Spirit.

THE HAND OF GOD IS A NECESSITY IN THE IMPLEMENTATION OF EVERY ASSIGNMENT

One of my favorite prayers is this: "Lord, if your hand is not upon it, please do not let me be part of it, near it, or go for it. Let something happen that will prevent me from going my way."

The hand of God sets captives free.

The Bible teaches us in Psalm 145:16 (NLT) that when God opens his hand, he satisfies the hunger and thirst of every living thing. It is his hand that will enable us to provide solutions to the people we encounter. It is not by our power but through his hand. It was by the hand of God that the Israelites got delivered from Egypt (Exodus 13).

IS YOUR ASSIGNMENT FACING AN "EGYPT-LIKE" SITUATION?

Then, pray for the hand of God to touch it. Let me share a quick story with you. Once upon a time, during the horrible recession that started in 2008, many people were afflicted with foreclosures and they lost homes, jobs, and more. Some people even committed suicide, and some attempted. In our situation, but for the hand of God, my husband and I would have been telling a different story today. Both of us were afflicted with unemployment at the same time. We had two children at the time; our son wasn't born yet. We carried mortgage payments, car notes, and everything else that goes with living the American dream.

They do say when it rains, it pours.

Prior to the unfortunate situation, we had decided that we were going to take the ministry one step further by starting a Bible study in our home. The date was set, and the invitations were sent out to other believers in the area.

On the eve of the inaugural Bible study, my husband was informed that his contract would not be renewed and before we knew what was happening, the economy tanked!

I had just had our second child, who was about three months old at the time. My mind started doing overtime. I went into survival mode and began applying for jobs everywhere. The reality of the economic downturn we faced was that everywhere we turned, more and more people faced the same issues. However, to the glory of God, our case was different. God saved us.

One day, as I was praying into the New Year, the Lord revealed 2 Kings 3:1-20 to me. It was one of those situations were the Scripture just stared at you with immediate divine revelation and you just knew that no matter what, everything would be fine.

WHEN THE HAND OF GOD TOUCHES A SITUATION, EVEN DESERTS BRING FORTH WATER

When the hand of God comes forth through worship, deep revelation takes place. The Scripture in 2 Kings 3:16-18 says that when the hand of the Lord came upon Prophet Elisha, he began to speak forth a divine solution that would turn drought to plenty.

> Thus says the LORD: "Make this valley full of ditches." For thus says the LORD: "You shall not see wind, nor shall you see rain; yet that valley shall be filled with water, so that you, your cattle, and your animals may drink." And this is a simple matter in the sight of the LORD; He will also deliver the Moabites into your hand.

Those Scripture verses saved us many years ago during the drought season. We became confident that even though we did not know how or where supply was going to come from, we were confident that because God said it, that meant he would do it.

And he surely did it!

In the wilderness of recession, our breakthrough came. You can read more about the story in my book, *The Bilhah Moment: How to Wait on God in Desperate Times*.

This was the period when houses were being foreclosed on by banks. There were times when I would drive home and would see summons notices on people's doors in the neighborhood. There were constant home auction announcements affixed to the wall at the local post office.

There was frustration everywhere, but we did not suffer loss.

The times were indeed frantic, but our living God did not fail us. A while back, I heard a man of God jokingly say that until you suffer disgrace in the name of the Lord, you have not started ministry. Should servants of God on assignment for him become embarrassed on the job?

Let's leave that alone for now, but understand this—there will be times when the devil will try, and even succeed, at doing things that will embarrass you. I have another story about that but you will read it in another book or hear it when you attend one of our conferences.

Look at us in that situation—the ministry name was already Persistent Faith Ministries. We were Bible study and prayer hosts who were teaching folks about faith and we did not have jobs.

It was as if the devil was saying, "Yeah, let's see how long you will last in this assignment that you have undertaken. You want to do Bible study? You want to pray right? Who will listen to you when you cannot even take care of yourself and your home?"

Our assignment in that season was *Bible Study* and *Prayer Meetings*. The consistent continuation despite financial lack required the hand of God. I must say that there were times when it would have been just easier to say, "Hello, everyone. We shall postpone the meetings until further notice. When we have jobs, we shall reconvene."

However, true character is revealed in trials and tribulations. How could we have halted the assignment because of what our bank account constantly showed us? The God who laid it in our hearts to do Bible study was definitely capable of supplying all our needs according to his riches in glory by Christ Jesus. And he did!

I shared this story for you to understand that when God's hand is upon your life and the assignment he gives you, he will protect and cover you. Your enemies will not laugh at you. You will not be the focus of laughter in the enemy's camp. The Lord satisfied our hunger and thirst. Was it a smooth ride? Absolutely not; but it was a destiny-defining moment.

As you continue with the implementation of your assignments, there will be high and low seasons. Remember 2 Kings 3:16-18. The God who has called you to do it will take care of you and your team. Just like the Scriptures say, you will not see any signs of provision coming (no wind, no rain), but you and your group will have water to drink. Thirst will not overcome you. God will provide for you.

Fourteen

DON'T WORRY ABOUT ATTACKS

Because you are called by God to carry out his assignments, expect some attacks. As a believer in the Lord Jesus Christ, you are already a target for Satan; but his plans will always fail, in Jesus' name.

Attacks can come from anywhere because he has a habit of injecting bad spirits into people to mess up your assignment. Have you ever experienced a situation where a close family member suddenly starts to act strangely towards you, knowing fully well that because of who you are, it would affect you?

I have. I know. And I dealt with it. By prayer and fasting.

I had one of my conferences coming up and some people who were close to me started acting like they were possessed by demons! I knew immediately where the attack was coming from because everything they requested from me at the time was totally out of alignment with God's plan for my life, a decoy from ministry and total disobedience to God.

To the physical eye, it could have been viewed as stubbornness, but with the spiritual eyes, it was very clear what the motive and mission was. At that time, the best thing I knew to do (which turned out to be awesome) was to take it to the Lord in prayer.

I am not talking about a quick prayer, even though that is helpful. It was a scheduled prayer session at a particular time for a set duration with one focus: the demonic and oppressive issue at hand.

And suddenly, everything stopped.

It is important to quickly recognize attacks and act accordingly. Every argument does not require a response. Sometimes silence is a great answer. It is golden. Just because you keep quiet does not mean you are foolish, either. The enemy knows our weaknesses and buttons to press to get God's servants to become easily distracted. Do not fall for it.

DON'T BE SURPRISED ABOUT HOUSEHOLD ENEMIES

In Matthew 10:36, Jesus said, "Your enemies will be right in your own household!" This is no surprise, because people who know a lot about you are most likely to discourage you from doing what you should do.

How can they dissuade you?

- By telling you: "I know you. You are not cut out for that stuff."
- By distracting you with their own problems and because of the depth of your relationship with them, most likely you will put your assignment on the back burner and go help take care of their business.
- By using manipulation and guilt trips to keep you bound.
- By constantly using tradition and customs to make you stay in a place where God has uprooted you from.

How does anyone know what you are cut out for? How do they know the extent of your capability in Christ Jesus? Doesn't the Bible teach us that we can do all things through Christ who strengthens us? Why should man, who is God's creation, now question the ability of another creation of God?

The spirit of manipulation can be used against you to get you to do what is abominable to God. In some cases, it is to distract you from your mission. In my walk and implementation of God's assignments, I have learned to develop thick skin and truly focus on what God has ordained.

Everybody will not agree with you. Everyone won't accept your philosophy. Has everything in my life always been smooth? Absolutely not. There were many rough roads, but God came through at every turn, and he continues to come through, in Jesus' name. If I should share my testimonies in this book, the pages would just be too many and it would take you a long time to finish it.

ABOUT FAMILY TIES AND CLOSE RELATIONSHIPS

Do not neglect your family, but your assignment requires total commitment. Some family members mean well and have our best interests at heart, but their best interests may not be God's plan for our lives. It is imperative that we constantly pray for discernment so we can make the right decisions. Our destinies cannot afford any mistakes, delays, or diversions.

The Message Bible version of Matthew 10:36-37 says:

> Well-meaning family members can be your worst enemies. If you prefer father or mother over me, you don't deserve me. If you prefer son or daughter over me, you don't deserve me.

If you ever find yourself in a situation that just does not feel right in your spirit, please pause. Take a break. Breathe in. Breathe out. Turn down the volume of any noise around you. Be still. Listen to the voice of the Holy Spirit. He reveals to redeem. He guides and saves.

Sometimes all we need to do is just keep quiet; do not sign any contracts or attach ourselves to any formalities and just wait. If you face attacks, do not be afraid. God, who has assigned you, will come through for you.

THE PAST FROM OLD WINESKINS MAY SHOW UP

Once in a while you may encounter reminders of your past, perhaps from people who know you or your history. Let me encourage you today to not give in to destiny-stealing reminders that have no place in your life.

It may be people you know, or even those close to you who do not believe that you are on a mission for the kingdom of God. Some will test you and really get on your nerves to see if you will retaliate in "the usual old way," but aren't they in for a big surprise? You will not fall for foolishness.

Didn't God use Apostle Paul mightily? He had a history. He murdered God's people yet he had a transformational divine experience on the road to Damascus. If he had allowed the reminders of his past to interfere with his assignments, do you know how many people would have received Jesus Christ as their Lord and Savior?

Consistently keep a clear conscience. Keep going on your ordained path, fully knowing that your past is over and the new you cannot be tainted with even the slightest stain. In Acts 24:16, Paul says, "I always try to maintain a clear conscience before God and all people." When you operate with a clear conscience, the enemy will try but he will always fail.

SETBACKS DO HAPPEN, BUT USE THEM TO COME BACK POWERFULLY

In my early conference planning days, there were setbacks. All the adverts went out, including social media marketing blasts. Even at church we had programs where people promised to attend but on that assigned day, they were nowhere to be seen. At some events only two or three people showed up in addition to my immediate family.

These setbacks were enough to make us quit, especially because of the huge financial investment involved in getting conferences, seminars and even the manpower together. However, I was constantly reminded by the Holy Spirit that the events are about destinies and I could not just quit! Instead of feeling disappointed, I stood on the Word in Romans 5:5 that says, "Hope does not put us to shame."

Whatever I do for the kingdom of God is about Jesus Christ, not me, and because I have hope in him, he won't disappoint. To God be the glory, the Lord has been faithful. When Christ is the focus and we set our eyes on things above, everything else will be added.

BEWARE OF TERRITORIAL SPIRITS ON THE WAY

Some people will not like you to enter their territories in your holy boldness. They have "ruled" the region for a long time, then suddenly you appear, walking and talking fearlessly and uprooting. You begin to operate with the kind of authority that cannot be fathomed. You are commanding things to happen and they are actually happening.

This craziness for Jesus that you have is plundering hell and destroying the enemy's camp. Do you think the enemy will just sit back and watch you continue without hindrance?

In Matthew 2, the Magi saw the star in the east and wanted to come and worship the baby born in Bethlehem, but King Herod did not like it. He was furious, and gave orders to kill all boys in Bethlehem and its vicinity who were two years old and under. He ruled the place. Why was this newborn baby suddenly so special? Herod operated with a territorial spirit.

A territorial spirit will do anything to ensure that its power is not taken or threatened. It is possible that you will experience it with pastors of churches who have some following but feel threatened by your assignment in their locale. I pray in the name of Jesus that you do not allow territorial spirits to block your assignment.

WATCH OUT FOR "CONVERTED" COMPANIONS

In your assignment journey, by the power of the Holy Ghost, some folks who convert and become born again may still have selfish motives. They will begin to follow you and accompany you on your assignments but beware. Every person who converts is not necessarily for you. He or she may even become a destiny threat.

> A man named Simon had been a sorcerer there for many years, amazing the people of Samaria and claiming to be someone great. Everyone, from the least to the greatest, often spoke of him as "the Great One—the Power of God." They listened closely to him because for a long time he had astounded them with his magic.
>
> But now the people believed Philip's message of Good News concerning the Kingdom of God and the name of Jesus Christ. As a result, many men and women were baptized. Then Simon himself believed and was baptized. He began following Philip wherever he went, and he was amazed by the signs and great miracles Philip performed.
>
> —Acts 8:9-13

Simon, who was a wizard, believed, got baptized, and followed Philip wherever he went. This was a man who did magic, and people thought he was using the power of God. He followed Philip because of the signs and wonders that God did through him. However, when you read the continuing verses in Acts 8:18-21, you will discover that he desired the power that Peter and John had.

"Let me have this power, too," he exclaimed, "so that when I lay my hands on people, they will receive the Holy Spirit!" But Peter replied, "May your money be destroyed with you for thinking God's gift can be bought!"

Simon's motive was clear and foolish. He thought he could buy power. His heart was not right before God. Baptism does not necessarily mean total conversion. This man followed men of God because he was enamored of the power and authority they operated with.

It is necessary for us (the assigned) to teach people on our journey that to be fully converted, old things must pass away and they too can operate with the same power and authority, with hearts that are in the right place.

Fifteen

YOUR ASSIGNMENT REQUIRES PERSISTENT FAITH

To implement your assignment, you need to be very persistent in your faith. Faith reverses situations. Faith transforms lives. Faith heals the sick. Faith gives favor in complex cases.

> A man came and knelt before Jesus and said, "Lord, have mercy on my son, because he has seizures and suffers terribly. He often falls into the fire or into the water. So I brought him to your disciples, but they couldn't heal him.
>
> Jesus replied, "You stubborn faithless people! How long must I be with you until you believe? How long must I put up with you? Bring the boy to me." Then Jesus rebuked the demon in the boy, and it left him. From that moment the boy was well.
>
> Afterward the disciples asked Jesus privately, "Why couldn't we cast out that demon?"

> "You didn't have enough faith," Jesus told them. "I assure you, even if you had faith as small as a mustard seed you could say to this mountain, 'Move from here to there,' and it would move. Nothing would be impossible."
>
> —Matthew 17:14-20

Faith is a necessary ingredient for life transformation. As believers, with Christ in us, the hope of glory, what is stopping us from really believing? The enemy has a field day when we fail to believe. In the situation with the demon-possessed boy, the faith of the disciples was not enough. For a metamorphosis of that caliber to occur, you must believe that what you say will actually happen.

In your assignment you will experience seasons of waiting, but do not be discouraged. In my own journey, I have since realized that the key to waiting on God is persistent faith. That is faith that does not give up; unshakeable and determined faith. There have been times of divine silence when I wondered if I was doing the right thing. In situations like that, I just submitted the issue to God and waited. However, waiting on God does not mean one should be idle. You must keep on going, producing, and God will take care of the rest.

LORD, GIVE US MORE FAITH

Often we pray, Lord, do this for me, Lord do that for me, but when do we pray, Lord, give me more faith? We need a lot of faith to do kingdom work. We need faith to win souls, because you will not always get a warm reception.

Once upon a time, I met a lady who attended our church but her adult daughter did not. I met the daughter in a grocery store one day and invited her to church. She responded with such annoyance that you would have thought that I was responsible for all her problems. She did not want to hear it. I eventually told her to have a nice day, wiped the dust off my feet, and moved on.

However, that encounter did not stop me from doing ministry. I am implementing assignments and by the grace of God, I continue to push forth. Although the lady gave me the cold treatment, the seed was planted and the invitation went forth. I left the rest to God, who takes care of his business.

PERSISTENT FAITH GIVES YOUR CASE SWIFT ATTENTION

To be successful in your assignment and to operate with peace of mind, your faith must be relentless.

Do you remember the story of the persistent widow in Luke 18:3-5? She needed justice in a dispute with her enemy but the judge on the case was wicked and he kept ignoring her. Her persistence became annoying to the wicked judge and he had no option but to answer her case.

> A widow of that city came to him repeatedly, saying, "Give me justice in this dispute with my enemy." The judge ignored her for a while, but finally he said to himself, "I don't fear God or care about people, but this woman is driving me crazy. I'm going to see that she gets justice, because she is wearing me out with her constant requests!"

Persistent faith reverses evil decisions and fixes bad behavior. The judge eventually heard the widow; how much more will our God do, who is ever-loving and kind?

> And will not [our just] God defend and avenge His elect [His chosen ones] who cry out to Him day and night? Will He delay [in providing justice] on their behalf? I tell you that He will defend and avenge them quickly. However, when the Son of Man comes, will He find [this kind of persistent] faith on the earth?"
>
> —Luke 18:7-8 (AMP)

No matter what you experience in life, whether in the implementation of your assignment or just dealing with life and the tests that come with it, remember to persist in your faith. God will hear your cry. Strive to operate with persistent faith and continue to believe that God will do what he says he will do.

FAITH CREATES RIPPLE EFFECTS

It is a key component in our lives. In an atmosphere where healing is already activated, by faith and by being present, you too can receive your own healing.

In Mark 5:21-29, Jairus, the leader of a synagogue, fell at the feet of Jesus and begged him to come and heal his daughter. As Jesus went with him along with the crowd, a woman who bled for twelve years heard about Jesus.

> So she came up behind him through the crowd and touched his robe. For she thought to herself, "If I can just touch his robe, I will be healed." Immediately the bleeding stopped, and she could feel in her body that she had been healed of her terrible condition.

The request for healing of Jairus' daughter was already in activation mode. The presence of Jesus was enough to get healed. She operated in faith and touched the hem of Jesus' garment and the bleeding stopped.

Her faith made her well. She believed. She did something about her belief—she took action and touched Jesus' garment. What she expected to happen did occur.

A similar thing happened to Bartimaeus, too, before he regained his sight. He had confident trust in the power of Jesus to erase blindness from his life and make him see again.

> Throwing his cloak aside, he jumped to his feet and came to Jesus. "What do you want me to do for you?" Jesus asked him. The blind man said, "Rabbi, I want to see."

"Go," said Jesus, "your faith has healed you." Immediately he received his sight and followed Jesus along the road.

—Mark 10:50-52 (NIV)

PERSISTENT FAITH GIVES BOLDNESS

The woman who previously hemorrhaged for twelve years and had to deal with the stigma was bold. She came up from the crowd and went behind Jesus and touched him. When you need something badly and you can see that the only one who can save you is right in front of you, timidity goes out the window and boldness takes over.

Your assignment requires persistent faith. You cannot operate without it. If you want to see results, you must have faith that has the audacity to proceed against all odds.

DON'T STOP AT ONLY THE MESSAGE

Strategy is required on your assignment. It is one thing to receive the message of the Lord Jesus Christ, but it is necessary to seal it with the baptism of the Holy Spirit, especially when you know that the people are ready to receive, the audience is captive.

> When the apostles in Jerusalem heard that the people of Samaria had accepted God's message, they sent Peter and John there. As soon as they arrived, they prayed for these new believers to receive the Holy Spirit. The Holy Spirit had not yet come upon any of them, for they had only been baptized in the name of the Lord Jesus. Then Peter and John laid their hands upon these believers, and they received the Holy Spirit.
>
> —Acts 8

SOME CO-LABORERS ARE APPOINTED TO FINISH

Why wasn't Philip the one the Lord used for baptism of the Holy Spirit to fall upon the people in Samaria? It was Peter and John who were sent. Sometimes your task in a region is just to initiate the first step and for other co-laborers to finish the task. The Lord's ways are not our ways. Do your part, and God will take care of the rest.

The Holy Spirit can come upon believers in any format the Lord chooses. For Peter and John, the strategy used for the Holy Spirit to come upon the people was prayer, then they laid their hands upon the believers. For such baptism to take place, they must first believe. They were believers who were ready to receive.

In Acts 10:34-44, Peter was teaching about the Good News of Jesus Christ to the Gentiles, reiterating what happened and the assignment given to those who believe in Christ. As he spoke, the Holy Spirit fell upon those who were listening.

There was no drama involved, no force, no gimmick, just God at work through his assigned in an ordained location. There is nothing that is happening now in ministry that has not happened before. Sometimes all we have to do is study how the apostles engaged audiences during their assignments and do what we must do.

YOU ARE QUALIFIED TO FINISH

I am excited that you have got to this point.

You have read all the chapters in this book.

I want you to understand that as the assigned of God, the implementation of the assignment will not always be easy or rosy, but with God on your side, you can do all things through Christ Jesus who strengthens us.

I strongly believe that what we confess with our mouths will happen. Now, I want you to repeat these words seven times:

I am qualified to finish.
I am qualified to finish.
I am qualified to finish.
I am qualified to finish.
I am qualified to finish.
I am qualified to finish.
I am qualified to finish.

AND YOU SHALL NOT BE MOVED

As you repeat the words, your confidence to carry out the assignment increases. As you carry out your assignments, opposition will arise; territorial spirits will rear their ugly heads, and those who have been benefitting from the absence of the true word of God will be determined to not let peace reign.

However, the blood of Jesus that was shed on Calvary for you and me is stronger than any evil power.

> Some itinerant Jewish exorcists who happened to be in town at the time tried their hand at what they assumed to be Paul's "game." They pronounced the name of the Master Jesus over victims of evil spirits, saying, "I command you by the Jesus preached by Paul!"
>
> The seven sons of a certain Sceva, a Jewish high priest, were trying to do this on a man when the evil spirit talked back: "I know Jesus and I've heard of Paul, but who are you?" Then the possessed man went berserk—jumped the exorcists, beat them up, and tore off their clothes. Naked and bloody, they got away as best they could.
>
> —Acts 19:13-16 (MSG)

Apparently, the news went round Ephesus about what happened, and that it was only God that could be behind it. Three fantastic things happened due to the foolishness of the sons of the Sceva, a Jewish high priest.

1. "A solemn fear descended on the city" (Acts 19:17 TLB). "The name of the Lord Jesus was greatly honored." There was reverence for his name.
2. People became curious about this Paul and what he preached.
3. Witches and warlocks surrendered their materials. "Many of the believers who had been practicing black magic confessed their

deeds and brought their incantation books and charms and burned them at a public bonfire" (Acts 19:18-19).

In your assignment you will encounter foolishness, but do not be offended. In the name of Jesus, whatever foolishness may arise in the progression of your assignment will be counterattacked by God Almighty. Any power that tries to copy the anointing or power that is in you shall be disgraced.

Seven is an important number in the Bible. Seal your statement by unfailingly repeating, "I am qualified to finish," seven times. Even if you started working on your assignment and something happened in your life that made you stall, it is time for you to rise up and finish it.

YOU ARE QUALIFIED TO FINISH

God did not push you out onto the earth to carry around a lot of unfinished business. You must finish what you started.

HERE'S MY PRAYER FOR YOU

I pray in the name of Jesus that you operate fearlessly in your assigned region and have a flourishing finish. The finisher's anointing is your portion, in Jesus' name. Unfinished business will not follow you, in Jesus' name. God will remove destiny interceptors from your path.

I pray in the name of Jesus that everything you do that concerns your assignment does not depart from Scripture.

> Now these are the gifts Christ gave to the church: the apostles, the prophets, the evangelists, and the pastors and teachers. Their responsibility is to equip God's people to do his work and build up the church, the body of Christ.
>
> —Ephesians 4:11-12 (NLT)

> And [His gifts to the church were varied and] He Himself appointed some as apostles [special messengers, representatives], some as prophets [who speak a new message from God to the people], some as evangelists [who spread the good news of salvation], and some as pastors and teachers [to shepherd and guide and instruct], [and He did this] to fully equip and perfect the saints (God's people) for works of service, to build up the body of Christ [the church].
>
> —Ephesians 4:11-12 (AMP)

As the assigned of God, by God, to carry out great exploits, I pray that you never depart from equipping the people of God to do his work in building up the body of Christ.

If you ever feel discouraged, please do not give up. Do not quit your assignment. Distractions can come from different places, including close family members, friends, and anyone who has access to you. When Job was down, it was his wife who mocked him that he should just curse God and die. The last thing one wants to experience if down is to be kicked in that situation.

> His wife said to him, "Are you still trying to maintain your integrity? Curse God and die."
>
> —Job 2:9 (NLT)

The Bible teaches us that this work should continue "until we all come to such unity in our faith and knowledge of God's Son that we will be mature in the Lord, measuring up to the full and complete standard of Christ" (Ephesians 4:13).

I pray that you operate with grace, and remember that we have a unified mission: *Christ revealed and Christ received.* That is, help people see Christ and help people receive Christ as their personal Lord and Savior.

May the Lord give you patience to do his work. May the Lord send destiny helpers to you; people genuinely ready to serve and help without any ulterior motives.

May the Lord protect you and those assigned to you from wolves in sheep's clothing, and may he set an impenetrable ring of fire around you and all that you do. May the Lord bless and keep you.

Now, go activate, implement, and create ripple effects. People are waiting for you. No more procrastination!

DESTINY REMINDERS AND QUOTES

by Belinda Enoma

Every platform isn't ordained for your feet. You don't have to be everywhere.

❦

Every "spiritual voice" isn't for your destiny.

❦

If you have been downgrading your gifts and talents, end it today. The problem with hiding your gifted glow is that you blur your authenticity, and you need it to fulfill your destiny.

❦

Learn to say no. It can save your life and protect your legacy.

❦

In your assignment, do not be afraid of witches and warlocks. The power of your assignment will make them surrender all their books of spells, incantations, and evil peripherals.

❦

Sometimes God will send you back to your roots so that others can see the transformative and elevating power of Christ in your life. However, discern the moment, because to be sent back on assignment does not mean to stay where he uprooted you.

There is power in your fingers. If your gift is writing, then write, because the world needs that deliverance via your fingertips.

Activate the Word you hear and read. You are already authorized to start and qualified to finish.

Seeking validation before activation of your assignment has consequences. Wise counsel is great, but disobedience to God - can your destiny afford the consequence?

Grace gives the audacity to say no. That is, if not for the grace of God, you would have dealt with things differently.

God can relocate you to activate your assignment. Sometimes, an elevated shift will not happen until you leave familiar surroundings.

Persistent faith is consistent, confident hope.

Divine direction is extremely important in the fulfillment of your destiny. Therefore, every invitation should not be accepted.

Fear God. Don't sell your birthright or destroy your seed because of desire for popularity or wealth.

Procrastination is not your friend. "Remember your Creator in the days of your youth" (Ecclesiastes 12:1) and do what you should do now while you are still young.

❦

The fulfillment of your destiny requires holy boldness. Either you are all in or all out. You cannot be in between. So, what is it going to be?

❦

Call a spade a spade. Manipulation is witchcraft. When someone is constantly trying to disrupt your destiny for his or her own selfish gain, it is manipulation. Jezebel was not called a witch for nothing. She was indeed very manipulative.

❦

Choose your mentor wisely so that you are not directed by a destiny interceptor.

❦

An activated purpose with the wrong strategy can lead to decades of frustration, unequally yoked collaborations, and even regret.

❦

When the Lord protects the destinies of his beloved, the plans of the enemy are intercepted for the glory of the Lord.

❦

You reap what you sow. If you sow discord, you shall reap it. If you sow peace, you shall reap it. Therefore, sow what you desire to reap.

ABOUT THE AUTHOR

Belinda Enoma is a renowned international speaker and destiny launcher. She is the founder of the global iEmancipateMe conference and several impactful ministry and marketplace events.
Meet her in a city near you.

www.istartandfinish.com
www.iemancipateme.com
www.persistentfaith.com

ASSIGNMENT JOURNAL

Made in the USA
Lexington, KY
05 July 2019